Cancelled

By Elisha Alexander Smith

"Cancelled": Calling off the hit that you've placed on your own life

Copyright © 2017 by Elisha Alexander Smith

We want to hear from you. Please send your comments about this book to: authorelisha@gmail.com

To contact the author or book an event, please email: authorelisha@gmail.com or call 678-371-2886

Cover Design - ISpeak Publishing Service
Interior Design - ISpeak Publishing Service
Editing - Make It Plain Ministries
Author Photo - Haigwood Studios - Roswell, GA.

All rights reserved. No part of this book may be reproduced, stored in a retrieved system, or transmitted in any form or by any means, electronic, mechanical, photocopying, recording, scanning, or otherwise, without the prior written permission of the author.

All Scriptures come from the New International Standard, International Version and the King James Version of the Holy Bible unless otherwise indicated. Take note that the name satan and related names are not capitalized. We choose not to acknowledge him, even to the point of violating grammatical rules.

Disclaimer

All the material contained in this book is provided for educational and informational purposes only. No responsibility can be taken for any results or outcomes resulting from the use of this material. While every attempt has been made to provide information that is both accurate and effective, the author does not assume any responsibility for the accuracy or use/misuse of this information.

Printed in the United States of America

ISBN 978-0-692-91050-4

WorTh Writing
Publishing Company

ISpeak Publishing Service
www.tiffanysgreene.com
www.ispeakpublishing.com
email: tiffanysgreene@gmail.com
Little Rock, AR.
501-519-6996

Worth Writing Publishing
Company Atlanta, GA.

THE PASTORS' REVIEWS

"This book by my daughter, Elisha Alexander Smith (in whom I am well pleased), is a sincere expression of her love and consideration for humanity. It is a coalescing of strength and beauty – strength of character, and beauty of compassion. The author shows her deep commitment to empowering all readers to live a fulfilled life. This is a book that I would highly recommend reading for practical life application."

Edward L. Alexander
Senior Pastor
Springfield, MO

"*Cancelled* addresses real-life struggles in a way that allows a person to remove the bandages from their wounds and find healing. The author provides a perfect balance of practical examples, coupled with profound insight on ways to access hope in the darkest areas of life. This book is ideal for book clubs, small group studies, or to share with someone who needs to be reminded of how much they MATTER. Although this book deals with dark and difficult subject matter, the author does an excellent job of leaving each reader feeling hopeful and uplifted."

Eric L. Alexander
Senior Pastor
North Little Rock, AR

"I want to personally thank God for my sister, Elisha Alexander Smith, for this amazing book. I appreciate the transparency and sincerity in all thirteen chapters. I believe each reader will appreciate it as well. This book has realigned and redefined so many areas in my own life in ways unimaginable. As a husband, father, son, brother, grandson, great-grandson, uncle, nephew, cousin, friend, pastor and leader, I've discovered (as a result of reading this book) that the person I matter to the most is God. I've failed at many things, but I'm not a failure … and neither are you. I believe every obstacle in my life was an opportunity for God to reach down, pick me up and say, 'My child, get up and look within. You've been off balance, but now I need you to stand tall because you matter to me.' You will be better and tremendously blessed by this book, knowing that what the devil meant for bad has already been *Cancelled*!"

Edrin L. Alexander
Senior Pastor
Memphis, TN

TABLE OF CONTENTS

ACKNOWLEDGMENTS ix

FOREWORD xi

INTRODUCTION 1

CHAPTER ONE   You Matter 5

CHAPTER TWO   Identity Crisis 11

CHAPTER THREE   Look Within 21

CHAPTER FOUR   The Shadow of Death 37

CHAPTER FIVE   Off Balance 47

CHAPTER SIX   Fragile: Handle with Care 55

CHAPTER SEVEN   Stand Tall 73

CHAPTER EIGHT   Seek Solitude 83

CHAPTER NINE   Swim Away 91

CHAPTER TEN   When the Wounds Won't Heal 99

CHAPTER ELEVEN   In Ruins 111

CHAPTER TWELVE   The Significance of the Cross 119

CHAPTER THIRTEEN   The Empty Grave 127

BIBLIOGRAPHY 135

ACKNOWLEDGMENTS

To My Husband Jason,

Thank you for your consistency. I've never had to look for you (physically or emotionally). You have always been right there every step of the way. Even when life was having its way with us, I can't remember a time when you checked out. You've seen me at my lowest moments, and loved me through them all. Thank you for covering me as I researched and wrote about this dark subject. The feeling I get when I wake up in the middle of the night, and hear you praying for me, is indescribable. I've never had a problem to which you didn't give your attention. You're a special kind of man! Thank you for supporting my vision as if it were your own. I appreciate you for being a man of peace, making it easy for me to get in a zone and write. There were many nights when you woke up with pens and paper stuck to you, but you never complained. You have the patience of Job. Thank you for encouraging me throughout this entire process and making me feel like everything I write is "worth writing." I am so grateful for you, and I thank God for loving me enough to give me a husband like you.

I love you forever,
Lisha

To Sirrod and Anijah,

You two could probably write a chapter in this book yourselves, just based on everything we've been through. We have had some tough days, but when I hear the two of you share childhood memories, they're always good. God has kept us! I'm grateful that our life changes have only made you two better. When you both were younger, there were days when I was just about to give up, but God used you both to remind me of why I had to keep going. You two motivated me then, and you still do now. Thank you for caring enough about my book–writing journey to share it with your friends. That means so much to me. Just know that this book is not only for everyone else, it's for the two of you as well. I pray that you live long, productive lives and always remember how much I love you both.

To Janiah and Josiah,

This book is for you two as well. It's guaranteed to help you understand how valuable you are to God. I may not have had the privilege of giving birth to you, but that sure doesn't make me love you any less. However, as much as I love you two, just know that God loves you more. Life won't be a piece of cake, but my prayer is that you never experience days as dark as the ones I've seen. Your future is bright, and I pray that it remains that way. Use this book as a tool, but always remember that God is the source of your strength. I love you. Live well!

And to Tiffany Greene-Moorer of Ispeak Publishing Services (publisher) and Helaine R. Williams of Make It Plain Ministries (editor), I thank you for helping me take the final steps to making this book a reality.

FOREWORD

Your life matters. Your life is valuable. Your life is necessary. You matter. You are important. You are valuable. Not simply because I say so, but because the architect, designer, and sustainer of your life says so.

Yes – God, Creator of the universe, also created and purposed you and has been sustaining you, as we see in Gen. 2-7 of the Holy Bible: *"Then the Lord God formed the man of dust from the ground, and breathed into his nostrils the breath of life, and the man became a living creature"* (English Standard Version). That means your life is not just another in a meaningless sea of souls. No, your life has been and is being meticulously fashioned by the God of life. You are not alone. You are not so broken that you are beyond repair. The darkness is not superior to the light. Cancel the voices in your head that tell you otherwise. Hear the words of life and light. Follow the path that leads to hope, and listen to those of us who care for your very soul.

In the King James translation of the Bible, the word "life" can be found about 450 times. See, God values life because He is the Creator and sustainer of life. And everything He has made, He loves. Everyone He has made, He walks with and fights for. Our enemy tries to deceive us into thinking that no one cares, that we are all alone, that no one really understands. He tries to make you feel that you're not that important and that you are not unique. All these are lies to make us feel as though our loving Maker is far from us. The truth is that God values your life, as we see in Acts 17:24-28 (ESV):

> **The God who made the world and everything in it, being Lord of heaven and earth, does not live in temples made by man, nor is he served by human hands, as though he needed anything, since he himself gives to all mankind life, and breath, and everything. And He made from one man every nation of mankind to live on all the face of the earth, having determined allotted periods and the boundaries of their dwelling place, that they should seek God, and perhaps feel their way toward him, and find him. Yet he is actually not far from each one of us, for "In Him we live, and move, and have our being"; as even some of your own poets have said, "For are indeed his offspring.'**

God is never far from any of us. We are His, and He takes care of His own. As we open our hearts to His Word and listen for His voice, our spirit reminds us that we were never alone. We have a genuine purpose. We are uniquely created and cared for. We remember that we were not made to go through this life alone; that we are joined to a calling much higher than anything this earth can offer. When we hear God's Word and run to it, it cancels the lies, deceit, and plan of hopelessness the enemy has for your soul.

Our heavenly Father not only cares for your life; He cares for the *quality* of your life: *"Keep your life free from love of money, and be content with what you have, for he has said, 'I will never leave you nor forsake you.' So you can confidently say, 'The Lord is my helper; I will not fear; what can man do to me?'"* (Hebrews 13:5-6, ESV). He sent His only Son into the world that we might have life, and have it more abundantly

(John10:10). This cancels the lies the enemy wants to use to take away your joy: The lie that nothing will ever go right in this life. The lie that life is full of cruelty. The lie that life will always keep you in the bottom of the bucket.

God didn't spend His time, energy, resources, thought and artistry creating you just to have you live ordinarily. No, He has a plan and purpose for you to live in the greater goodness of His creation! This doesn't refer to material possessions. It's more about taking you to a place where the intangible fruits of life – true love, true joy, true fellowship, true contentment, a true feeling of belonging – are enjoyed in the abundance in which God ordained for you to abound. That way, regardless of where life may take you, there are fruits inside of you that are secured in heaven and therefore can't be taken away.

The wonderful light you are about to bring to your life via the following pages is designed to guide you to the abundant life God has designed and purposed for you. The bountiful blessings wrapped in these chapters will minister to those who feel self-destruction is their only path to relief and peace. As you read, it is important to note that this could be any person, anytime, anywhere. It is deception to think that you are the only person who has ever needed the healing balm this work of art has to offer. We all have had moments where we felt we needed more than just another sermon, church service, or book. Every person has lived a moment of crying out for the real, manifest glory of God's presence to flood our room and hearts, and to hold us. You are not alone.

As we are all unique, I am not going to assume I know exactly what you are going through. I can beg you, plead with you, and implore you to not fall for the hit the enemy has you placing on your life and forfeit the abundant life for which God has made you. I plead as someone who has been left behind by a loved one who wrestled with the dark stains of suicide and hopelessness. Many in this place are deceived by the enemy. He will try to make you believe that no one will care what happens to you.

The idea that maybe others will be better off without you is a misunderstanding of others' need for you. God has fashioned our lives uniquely; He has designed our lives to be interwoven with others' lives. Yes, you have been created with gifts that others need, and they have been created with gifts you need. And since our Creator made us in this way, there will never be a time, other than when He calls you home, that others will be better off without you.

People like myself, dealing with the incompleteness of life due to the loss of a loved one to suicide, are left to pick up pieces that were only fulfilled by the lost loved one. I miss my mother every day. There are many times I wish I could tell her how much she completed me, and that I am NOT better off without her. I wish my children could meet their grandmother (my mom). I wish I could have brought my wife home to her while we were dating, and that they could have developed a relationship. I wish I could show her all these pieces in my life's puzzle that are incomplete without her here. What I *can* do is share with countless others, as I have since 2005, in hopes of getting anyone contemplating this path of hopelessness to see their unique purpose and value, their need for others, and most of all, others' need for them.

I am excited about the glory God will receive from the obedience of Elisha Alexander Smith. God's glory in this effort will lead to the restoration of many. The ministry of this book should not be seen as only for those currently contemplating suicide. It should be seen as a resource for the body of Christ as a whole.

Listen, BOC (body of Christ), this is part of learning to *"weep with them that weep"* (Romans 12:15). Catch the vision of this ministry that comes through the art of writing, and become a beacon of hope for someone in a dark place. If you are someone reading this treasure because you are in a battle with the deception of self-harm or suicide, I encourage you to read it along with another believer or in an accountability group, where you can be strengthened among those who can love you through the hurt to hope.

I believe anyone who reads this work, whether battling self-harm/suicide or not, will come out with a better understanding of God's view and value of all lives (black, white, Hispanic, Jewish, Middle Eastern, etc., born or unborn) and the understanding that God intentionally created us to need each other. Elisha Alexander-Smith, thanks for your act of sacrifice and obedience in reaching others and leading them to life. I can't wait to see the emails and letters from readers saying, "Hit cancelled."

Christopher T. Cross
Visionary and Lead Pastor
Christ Community Missional Fellowship
Jacksonville, AR

INTRODUCTION

It was a beautiful Wednesday afternoon, April 25, 2012. The sun was shining brightly and the sky was as clear as could be. I had just left a lunch date with my husband, Jason. I remember driving and reflecting on the conversation we'd just had (like I always did), not knowing that after this day I would never again see life the same way.

While heading northbound on Interstate 430 in Little Rock, I noticed that traffic was unusually heavy for this time of day. As I reached the bridge that spans the Arkansas River, I could see a swarm of people at the north end. I'd made it about halfway across when I spotted what appeared to be a young man standing on the railing of the bridge. I think my heart stopped for a moment. *If I could just get to him,* I thought to myself.

My adrenaline kicked in. Although the traffic was heavy, I managed to maneuver my way to the shoulder of the interstate. I jumped out of my vehicle, and despite a partially dislocated knee, I ran and ran and ran ... almost a half-mile. As I was running, I realized that the person standing on the bridge railing was, in fact, a young boy. I could hear people asking him if he could swim. He responded "No, I can't." At this point, I'm thinking, *Somebody just grab him, and stop asking questions.* As I ran, I kept yelling, "Don't jump! Don't Jump! God, please don't let him jump!"

I was no more than thirty feet away from the boy when ... he jumped! I screamed out frantically, "Oh God, *NO!*" I tried running down the side of the bridge toward the riverbank, but the state troopers had already made it down there and would not let anyone by. In my mind, I could save this young boy. I saw him struggling to bring himself above water. His hands came up a couple of times, then he disappeared. (He didn't come back up until the next day, when his body was recovered.)

It seemed like a very bad dream. As traffic moved slowly past, I sat down on the concrete bridge in total disbelief. I had never witnessed anything so tragic. The sadness and sorrow you feel after watching someone take their life is indescribable. The feeling of hopeless grief completely overtakes you.

My sincere desire is that after reading *Cancelled*, you'll understand the connection between the pain in your life and the purpose for your life. My prayer is that you'll know without a doubt how valuable you are to God, and know the importance of your existence here on earth. My sole purpose for writing this book is to serve notice on the enemy, confronting the source of destruction head-on. I encourage you to live out the plan that God has for you. He has created you to fulfill a specific role in this world.

There is no one else who can carry out what God has purposely created you to do.

Regardless of who you are or where you come from ... you deserve to live. You are needed, and you are loved. You are not an accident. Nothing regarding your existence is superficial. You are valuable, significant, and worthy of thought and concern. The world may not always affirm this. Your friends and family may not appropriately communicate the importance of your presence. But it doesn't mean that who you are, and what you do, doesn't have a deeply-felt impact on the world.

A Note from the Author

If you look up the word "suicide" in any thesaurus, you'll find the word "self-destruction." When you hear of someone who is self-destructive, you typically think of a person who lives a reckless life, using drugs or alcohol or maybe even engaging in sexual promiscuity. While this behavior is damaging, there are so many ways to self-destruct other than the obvious. You may not kill yourself in the literal sense, but if you are constantly harboring, hate, bitterness, resentment or any other unhealthy emotion, you're killing something *in* and *around* you. These feelings are detrimental because they're so easily hidden. You can't look at a person and tell that they haven't forgiven someone, nor can you tell that they are living in self-blame. These emotions are diseases of the soul from which only God can deliver you.

God has a purpose for each of us to live out. Mistreating yourself and others was *never* a part of the plan. As you read, open your heart, and let God in, a life of fulfillment awaits you.

– 1 –
YOU MATTER

Even before he made the world, God loved us and chose us in Christ to be holy and without fault in his eyes.

(Ephesians 1:4, NLT)

I've always known how important it is to love everyone else, but it took decades for me to understand how crucial it was for me to consider myself ... my heart ... my feelings ... my thoughts ... my well-being. Throughout life, I justified so many things that were said and done to me because of my lack of self-love. I made allowances not only for what others said and did to me, but also for the mean things I said and did to *myself*. I had a way of sentencing myself like no one else could. Somehow, the enemy that lived inside of me had convinced me that I deserved every hurtful thing that had ever happened to me.

I was a thirty-year-old, divorced mother of two when I realized I mattered. It was like turning on all the lights in a pitch-black house! I suddenly realized that the darkness had kept me from seeing things that were always there, such as my dreams, my desires, my passion. I could see so much clearer. My heart and my eyes were open to *give* love, and *receive* it. The cold, uneasy feeling that the dark brings was no longer there. Since that moment I've never seen God, or myself, the same way.

You'll read thousands of words in this book, but there are two that I want you to remember the most. And they are ... **You matter**!

I believe this clear, simple message is the antidote for much of the tragedy and suffering that saturate our world today – the shootings, the hatred, the suicides. To every man, woman, child, teacher, preacher, pastor, and leader: You matter! Your life, and what you do with it, matters. You are indispensable to God's vision of the world. You were chosen to fulfill an assignment in this world that only you can accomplish. You matter not because you think you're important, or because others tell you that you are; you matter not because of your financial status, looks, mood, performance, or productivity. What I'm saying is that you are *necessary*. You are irreplaceable. Period.

Some of us are infested with lies that were deeply imbedded in our spirits. Most of the lies are not from others; they are lies we have told ourselves. The most common lie is that "something is wrong with me." The belief that you are insufficient is the main ingredient of personal shame. Unfortunately, we are encouraged by society to compare ourselves to others and obsess over whether we're prettier, uglier, taller, shorter, lighter, darker, smarter, or dumber. Usually we see ourselves as the ones who fall short. These beliefs are often internalized – we tell ourselves that we aren't good enough the way we are; that we are significantly flawed; that we are unlovable. We begin to resent, and reject, whatever distinguishes us from others. (If you've had a disturbing and traumatizing past, you will most likely own these thoughts more than others. It can be tough, but you must learn to forgive yourself as well as anyone responsible for the pain of your past.)

When you know that you and your contribution to life are crucial, it infuses you with a compelling sense of urgency. On the other hand, when you feel that neither you nor your actions matter, you lose your motivation to care for the lives of others as well as your own. The clutching belief that you are somehow deficient undermines everything you think and do and gives misery access in and throughout your life.

What's odd is that we're afraid to let go of the belief that we're substantially deficient. Why is that? Why do we hold on to the idea that we are somehow subhuman? We tell ourselves lies such as: "I'm not worthy of the same love and success as others" or "I have nothing to offer, and I'm completely irrelevant." Because this is the only identity you know, you hold on to your misery and wear it like a badge of honor.

Be careful to not let your inner critic speak louder than the truth. Your inner critic will quickly create doubts and fears in your mind, and cause you to become blind to your own amazing opportunities. Most of all, your inner critic ultimately crushes your self-confidence and leaves you looking for it everywhere except the place that you'll find it – within yourself. That's right: Your self-confidence lives inside you. It does not deplete itself or run away and desert you. It's a permanent part of who you are. It's how God created each of us.

> *Be careful to not let your inner critic speak louder than the truth.*

Learn to tune out the negative voices and replace them with the truth of God's Word. God loves you and thinks the world of you. You're the apple of His eye. When you *believe* you are valuable in God's sight, you'll start *acting* like it. You will state it with assurance and set boundaries so that people will treat you with the dignity befitting a person made in God's image.

Perhaps you've been looking for your identity in the approval of others, or in your performance … your role at church, work, or home. Remember that no single facet of your life determines your worth. Now is the time to transition from finding out who you are in what you do to finding out who you are in Christ.

Knowing how important you are to God will change the course of your life. He created you not because He needed you, but because He *wants* you. God existed in perfect love and unity before He even created time. He didn't make you because He needed His ego fed, nor did He make you to satisfy some craving to be worshipped. God is totally secure in who He is without you! Despite not needing you, God chose to create you anyway. He wants you. God created you for His plan, His purpose, and His pleasure. The world would be different if you were not here, or if you do not fulfill your calling.

You have been given a unique set of gifts and talents. There are places you will go and experiences you will have, and in these settings will be people you will meet. They are assigned to you in order for you to use your gifts and talents to transform them, leaving them much different and much better than how you found them. It's called living with a purpose and making an impact on others. You were born to change someone's life forever. Being present is a big deal. Your presence is the most important contribution you can make.

You matter to God, and just as you matter to God, every person you encounter should matter to you.

PRAYER
"YOU MATTER"

Dear Lord,

Thank You for revealing to me how valuable I am. Your Word reaffirms to me daily what You think of me. I pray that I will continue to see how much I matter. Help me to tune out the inner critic and listen for Your voice. When the enemy tries to get me to feel worthless, remind me of who YOU say that I am. I'm confident that my life has meaning and purpose. Thank You for sacrificing Your life at Calvary … Your biggest demonstration to me that I matter. Amen.

– 2 –
IDENTITY CRISIS

But you are a chosen people, a royal priesthood, a holy nation, God's special possession, that you may declare the praises of him who called you out of darkness into his wonderful light.

(1 Peter 2:9, NIV)

If someone walked up to you and asked, "Who are you?", how would you respond? Most of us would simply give our name. Have you thought about who you really are … not who you *want* to be, or who *society* thinks you are, but your *own* definition of you? Some people have such a distorted idea of themselves that when they look in the mirror, they don't even recognize who's looking back. They are miserable in their own skin because of an unformed identity.

When you are shaped by what's around you rather than your own beliefs and personality, that's an indication of an identity crisis. When you lack a sense of who you are, it prevents you from knowing who you'll become. There are men, women, boys and girls all over the world who base their interests on what someone else likes or dislikes – even down to their appearance and demeanor. Often, the problem with a relationship is that it consists of two people trying to learn about *each other* despite having spent inadequate time getting to know *themselves*.

Each of us has an inner self that's longing to be revealed. It's frustrating when the "real you" is trapped inside! It causes stress and anxiety. I read a quote once: "There is no need to know exactly who you are to do well in life." I completely disagree. I believe the only way to truly do well in life is to know exactly who you are! Without having a clear sense of who you are, you'll never know the power you possess.

Many therapists suggest strategies to help you find a sense of identity. Talk therapy and psychotherapy are among them. I am certainly not opposed to seeking professional help. In many cases, it's crucial. However, as a Christian, you must realize that the only way to know for sure who *you* are is to know who *God* is. Your identity is not determined by what you do or what you've done, but who God says you are. Understanding your identity in Christ is crucial to living life as God intended. The more you grasp this, the more your behavior looks like God.

The characteristics of God are immeasurable. I've listed many of them (along with a scripture reference) to give you a better understanding of who God really is:

Advocate – 1 John 2:1	A Mighty God – Rev. 11:17
Alpha & Omega – Rev. 1:8	All Sufficient – Ps. 46
Author & Finisher of Our Faith Heb. 12:2	A Sun & Shield – Ps. 84:11
A Present Help in Trouble – Ps. 46:1	Blessed Hope – Titus 2:13
Comforter – John 14:26	Counselor – Is. 9:6
Deliverer – Rom. 11:26	Door – John 10:9
Faithful & True – Rev. 3:14	Father of Mercies – 2 Cor. 1:3
A Sure Foundation – Is. 33:6	Fountain/Living Water – John 4:14
God Alone – Ps. 86:10	God Full of Compassion – Ps.103:8
God of Love & Peace – 2 Cor. 13:11	God Our Rock – Ps. 18:2
Immanuel – Is. 7:14	Lamb of God – John 1:29

Now that you've had a closer look at who God is, declare who you are in Him (without formulating your identity on a person or an affiliation).

> *For too long, however, we have based our identity on the church, and not on the Savior.*

Like many Christians, I am a lover of the church; she's the bride of Jesus Christ. For too long, however, we have based our identity on the church, and not on the Savior. When you know who you are, you become a better leader, husband, wife, child, parent, friend. You become a better YOU!

Forty-three "I Am" Declarations

Forty-three is the biblical number of contention. Contention is strife in debate; dispute; and a point affirmed in controversy. It is my hope that these declarations will end the debate you may be experiencing internally.

1. **I am a child of God**
2. **I am redeemed from the hand of the enemy**
3. **I am forgiven**
4. **I am saved by grace through faith**
5. **I am justified**
6. **I am sanctified**
7. **I am a new creature in Christ Jesus**
8. **I am strong in the Lord**
9. **I am covered**
10. **I am delivered from the power of darkness**
11. **I am led by God**

12. I am kept
13. I am walking in favor
14. I am getting all my needs met
15. I am casting all my cares on Jesus
16. I am powerful with God
17. I am confident
18. I am valuable
19. I am an heir of God
20. I am obeying God
21. I am blessed going in and blessed coming out
22. I am protected
23. I am better than blessed
24. I am healed
25. I am above and not beneath
26. I am more than a conqueror
27. I am an overcomer
28. I am defeating the enemy
29. I am not moved by what I see
30. I walk by faith, and not by sight
31. I am casting down satan's plot
32. I am living for God
33. I am being transformed
34. I am winning
35. I am staying with God

36. **I am the righteousness of God**
37. **I am the light of the world**
38. **I am blessing the Lord at all times**
39. **I am the head and not the tail**
40. **I am putting on the mind of Christ**
41. **I am blessing my family and friends**
42. **I am trusting God daily**
43. **I am free from all bondages**

Since we belong to Him, we should follow Him.

Follow the Shepherd

"Know that the LORD is God. It is he who made us, and we are his; we are his people, the sheep of his pasture." (Psalm 100:3, NIV)

Many of us become lost when we drift away from the shepherd. We put ourselves in the most dangerous position imaginable. Whether you wander off on your own or follow someone else who is lost, you are unsafe.

Sheep have been branded as dumb when in fact, they are highly intelligent. Since a sheep is considered a dumb animal, I've always wondered about the connection between Christians and sheep. So, I decided to research sheep behavior. What I learned was astounding: A sheep's behavior is more like human behavior than I ever imagined! My study revealed how important it is for both types of sheep to have a strong shepherd/leader.

The Sheep

According to information at Followyourdreamfarm.net, sheep's eyes are set on the sides of their heads. They can't see in front of them, but they have perfect peripheral vision. They can see behind them without turning their heads. Just like some of us, sheep are easily distracted by what's going on behind them and on the side of them. Sheep are reluctant to go where they can't see. I'm sure this is why a pastor or leader has such a tough time getting the flock to follow the vision! The sheep can't see it, so they're very hesitant to embrace it.

In addition, sheep have a strong instinct to follow the sheep in front of them. When one sheep moves, the rest will follow – even if it's not a good idea. Sound familiar? In 2005, about 450 sheep were killed in Turkey following a sheep that jumped off a cliff. More would have died, except for the fact that their falls were cushioned by the bodies of the dead sheep! Many of us follow people who are just as lost as we are. We follow them because they *look* like they know where they're going.

Sheep are highly preyed-upon animals, so they become stressed and agitated if separated from the flock. Because sheep travel in herds, it's harder for the predator to pick them out. Although the enemy is already after you, you won't be such an easy target if you stay under your covering and stay connected to the body of Christ.

Healthy sheep are always hungry and eager to eat. They seek out food and cry out in anticipation to be fed. They rapidly approach the feeding area. They chew for hours. That's what we as Christians should do ... chew on the Word all day and all week. Eating makes sheep friendlier and less intimidated by people. Do you know someone who is always paranoid and suspicious of everyone? This person needs to chew on the Word so that he will know God has not given him the spirit of fear, but of power, love, and a sound mind.

If you are a Christian who has lost your appetite for the Word of God, this is an indication that something is seriously wrong. You need to pray and ask the Great Physician to examine you. Ask Him to search your heart to see what's keeping you from being hungry for His Word: *"Search me, O God, and know my heart; test me and know my anxious thoughts. Point out anything in me that offends you, and lead me along the path of everlasting life"* (Psalm 139:23-24, NLT).

When you are full of everything else, you won't hunger for God's Word.

As a mother, I recall many days that I told my children they could not eat sweets before their meal. I knew they would lose their appetite. When you are full of everything else, you won't hunger for God's Word. Some of us are so busy that we *forget* to eat. We're slowly killing ourselves, walking around spiritually malnourished. However, a good sheep knows how to self-medicate.

When a sheep wanders, it's a sign that it's sick or in pain. Another reason sheep sometimes wander off is because they are jealous of one another. They carry emotional baggage. (It may take us human "sheep" years, sometimes a lifetime, to heal from traumatic experiences.)

Last, but not least, sheep grieve for their lost loved ones and cry out in a desperate attempt to understand why they are not there. As Christians, we should always be moved, and bothered, when other Christians (sheep) fall off. We should do what "healthy" sheep do ... desperately try to figure out why they are missing.

Now, I realize some people have problems that are perceived rather than real. The reason they are absent may simply be a figment of their own imagination. They *think* someone doesn't like them, or they *think* people are talking about them. Nonetheless, we should always reach out and make every attempt to gain an understanding of a fellow sheep's pain. Your thoughtfulness might give that person the needed hope to keep living and become reunited with the flock. Don't ever become comfortable with the fact that a sheep is lost!

Prayer

"Identity Crisis"

Dear Lord,

Thank You for the knowledge and understanding of Your Word. It's because of You that I no longer have an identity crisis. I know who I am and *whose* I am. Thank You for calling me daughter (son). Draw me closer to You. I want to look like You, walk like You, and be like You. Give me the boldness to declare every day who I am in You. Thank You for choosing me and making me feel so loved by You. You are such a good Father. I don't deserve You, or Your love, so I'm forever grateful. Help me to let my light shine so bright that people who don't know You will see You, and learn of You through me. Amen.

– 3 –
LOOK WITHIN

Get rid of all bitterness, rage, anger, harsh words, and slander, as well as all types of evil behavior.

(Ephesians 4:31, NLT)

Twin Terrors (Guilt and Shame)

Romans 8:1 tell us, *"There is therefore now no condemnation to them which are in Christ Jesus, who walk not after the flesh, but after the spirit"* (KJV). But all too often, guilt and shame cause us to forget this Biblical assurance.

Guilt and shame rob us of our peace, freedom, and happiness. When someone makes you feel guilty or ashamed, and you place blame on yourself, you go through an enormous amount of unnecessary suffering. Guilt and shame are nearly identical, but they have their differences. It's possible to feel guilt without feeling shame, but you can't feel shame without feeling guilt. For instance, when you feel guilt, you say: "I made a mistake." When you feel shame, you say: "I *am* a mistake."

> *Too much self-condemnation will make you feel bad without ever solving the problem.*

I believe it's healthy to regret causing pain and to take full responsibility for your actions, but self-blame and self-criticism is completely unhealthy. Too much self-condemnation will make you feel bad without ever solving the problem. Many doctors and therapists say guilt is a healthy emotion. I totally agree. However, we should always walk in faith, not regret. There is absolutely nothing wrong with feeling remorseful. You *should* feel that way. But just as the person who was done wrong should forgive you, you should forgive yourself as well. Many times, we feel as though we haven't been sufficiently punished.

You must get to a place where you understand that **God does not need help being your Father!** Every time you self-sabotage because of guilt and shame, you become a terrorist of your own soul. It's like hijacking yourself, holding up your own peace and freedom. Make the decision to free yourself. Never become a prisoner of your emotions. You must be careful not to allow guilt and shame to overtake you. Your self-esteem is at stake. More important, your LIFE is at stake.

Here's a list of things that can lead to feelings of guilt and shame.

Parenting issues

Poor financial status

Abortion

Abnormal weight/poor health

Infidelity

Rape/molestation

Homosexuality

Lack of education

Death ("would've, could've, should've" survivor's guilt)

There are four questions you should ask yourself if you feel guilt or shame:

1. **What am I blaming myself for?**
2. **Why am I blaming myself?**

3. **Am I taking on someone else's responsibility, or is it really my own?**

4. **How's it working for me? (Yes ...** *Ask yourself* **the question Dr. Phil asks subjects on his talk show.)**

Feeling guilt is like having a cold, but feeling shame is like having the flu. The effects are much more severe; they can, in fact, even be deadly. Shame is debilitating. It wears you down. It causes your strength to diminish; you become weak emotionally, spiritually, and physically. Pay attention! Don't let the twin terrors creep in and destroy your life. Remember, if you make a mistake or something bad happens to you, be careful not to turn your pain and anger inward. If you haven't done so already, ask God to help you take control of your emotions before they take control of you. Just know that with God, all things are possible.

Feeling guilt is like having a cold, but feeling shame is like having the flu.

During those times in life when the twin terrors come to overtake you, remember that there are another set of twins – grace and mercy. These twins cancel out guilt and shame. Grace and mercy are powerful! The only reason you are still here today is because of God's grace and mercy. Guilt and shame causes us to convict and sentence ourselves to death.

Despite what we have done, grace overpowers our magnified sin, and mercy overlooks it.

Keep in mind that God sees things differently. **Despite what we have done, grace overpowers our magnified sin, and mercy overlooks it.**

Let Yourself Off the Hook

Even harder than forgiving someone else is forgiving yourself. Throughout life, we make choices of which we are not always proud. These choices leave us feeling embarrassed and disappointed – so much so that we hold grudges with ourselves. These self-directed grudges cause us to ignore our own needs. We tell ourselves things like "I don't deserve to be happy," "It's my fault that I'm miserable," "I hate myself," or "I hate my life."

It doesn't matter whether you contributed to your pain or not – it's not your job to make sure you suffer. You don't belong to you. You're a child of the King, redeemed from the hand of the enemy ... even if the enemy is you. How would you feel if your child was living a reckless life without care, concern or caution? If your child was hurting himself or herself, would that not bother you? Imagine what God thinks when He sees His children punishing themselves for mistakes/sins that He has already forgiven.

It doesn't matter whether you contributed to your pain or not – it's not your job to make sure you suffer.

The liberation that comes from forgiveness is phenomenal! Instead of using your energy to harbor resentment and self-hate, use it to become a better person. Holding a grudge with yourself or anyone else is exhausting. The longer you foster the grudge, the harder it will be for you to have a positive outlook on life. Negativity will consume you. Consistent resentment causes bitterness, and bitterness is like gangrene. Gangrene is a medical term used to describe the death of an area of the body. Just like gangrene, bitterness causes you to be cold and numb. Bitterness eats away at your heart and soul. It's not your average disease. It's a disease of the spirit that will ruin any chance you have to enjoy relationships, or even life itself. It's toxic and lethal. Not only will bitterness destroy your ability to enjoy relationships, it will keep others from enjoying a relationship with you. Give yourself a chance to give love, and receive it as well.

The Severity of Bitterness

If you have not dealt with emotions such as anger, resentment and unforgiveness, they can easily lead to bitterness. Bitterness is like a toxic gas that seeps through the cracks of your home. You may not even detect it because you have become so accustomed to the scent. If someone else comes around, however, they'll detect it immediately.

I want to give you a clear understanding of bitterness, so let me give you another example. Think of bitterness as Stage Four cancer. You're the one with the deadly illness, but you're not the only one affected by it. It alters the lives of everyone close to you – spouse, children, parents, and friends. They want to help you, but it's beyond their ability.

The Root

I love working in my yard. It takes a lot of effort, but I'm always pleased with the results. The hardest part is keeping the weeds under control. Weed killer is helpful, but if it gets on the healthy grass and plants, it could kill them. After using a number of chemicals, I discovered that the only way to truly get rid of weeds is to pull them up at the root. Cutting them down or spraying them only keeps them from being visible. I'd be leaving behind the part that keeps them growing!

The more the weed grows, the more the root grows. For instance, if you have a tree in *your* yard, the roots have probably reached your *neighbor's* yard. Roots run deep and wide. As strange as it seems, the most important part of the tree is the part that you can't see. What you see above ground is determined by what's hidden underground.

Roots are the lifeline of a plant or tree. They provide water and other nutrients that keep the tree alive. My question to you is: What's keeping your tree alive? Is it your resentment toward someone? If you have become bitter, it's a direct result of a past hurt or offense that you haven't forgiven. You'll use what happened to you to justify your negative actions. For example, if you were in a relationship and it ended against your wishes, you could be harboring R.A.B.U. (resentment, anger, bitterness, and unforgiveness) without being aware of it. Or you might know exactly what your issue is but, as I stated before, you're finding ways to justify how you act and feel. When a tree is planted, it could take weeks, sometimes months, for the root to settle in the ground. Water and fertilizer speeds up this process.

When someone has hurt you, address the issue … take it to God right away. Don't give bitterness a chance to catch root. Every time you condone your unhealthy behavior, you are fertilizing that "bitterness root," causing it to grow at an accelerated speed. Once it takes off, it's gone! The only way to stop it is to pull up the root. In my opinion, bitterness is the worst of all destructive behaviors. I say that because bitterness comes after all the other unhealthy emotions are out of control. It's like a tooth with a cavity that is beyond needing a filling. The decay has gone deep into the nerve and the root. The only solution is to get a root canal, or pull the tooth before the infection spreads.

Most people will never admit that they are bitter, even after they have been made aware of their behavior. If you ever want to see someone come unglued, call them bitter! No one wants to be called bitter, even those who feel they have good reason to be. The strange thing is that despite how bad their bitterness may sound to *them*, people hardly ever seem to put forth the effort to *end* their bitterness. I realize that bitterness is not something that can simply be wiped away. But the attempt must be made.

Addressing bitterness can be painful because you must find the root, and pain will always be found wherever the root is. I call this the "sore spot." In order to put an end to bitterness, you must revisit the sore spots. It can be devastating to even go near them, but it's necessary for healing to begin.

Take a look at the sore spots I have listed below. When you find yours, stop reading and start praying. Don't wait until you've finished the book. Get in a habit of urgently seeking God.

- **Divorce/Broken Relationship**
- **Molestation/Rape**
- **Abandonment by Mother or Father**
- **Death of a Loved One**
- **Sibling Conflict/Family Discord**
- **Best Friend Betrayal**
- **Exposure/Scarred Reputation**

You have to let yourself "go there." Ignoring the hurt and acting as if the violation never happened will not help. It will only make matters worse.

Bitterness grows and eventually becomes overpowering … just like roots. Some trees and plants have roots that are no longer hidden because they began to grow above ground. If you don't address this destructive behavior, it will soon become impossible to hide. Everyone around you will notice. The bitterness will cause your insides to rot, and will quickly spread to the outside. Your foul attitude will bring negative energy to every room you enter. No one will want to be in your company. The only people who will enjoy being around you are other bitter people.

A bitter person will find something wrong with *everything* and be suspicious of *everyone*. If you're bitter and like to hang out with other bitter people, just know that your bitter buddies will eventually find something wrong with you, too!

Pulling the Root: The Process

1. **Go back to the day of the offense.**
2. **Accept that it happened.**
3. **Admit that it still hurts.**
4. **Get rid of the victim mentality.**
5. **Make the decision to LET IT GO!**
6. **Forgive the person who hurt you (even if they're not remorseful).**
7. **Forgive yourself.**
8. **Live a productive life.**

Remember that what you do with your hurt is more important than the hurt itself.

> *Remember that what you do with your hurt is more important than the hurt itself.*

Made Straight

In Luke 13:10-13, Jesus was preaching in the synagogue. Among those present was a woman who was crippled, bent over for eighteen years. Not only was she bent over; her body was twisted. In that time, a twisted body identified a person as full of ignorance, malice, anger and hopelessness – one who could only see negative things. This woman could only look down. She was only able to see filth. Her condition would not allow her to look upward. The woman's body was overtaken by a spirit. Now this is what happens when a person is consumed by bitterness. It's impossible for them to look up. They can only see what's wrong. Not only do they see the bad in everyone else, they can only see the bad in themselves. They can't even see the possibilities that are right before them.

Bitterness is a beast, but it's no match for Christ! This woman had been crippled for eighteen years, but it only took a moment for her to be healed. Jesus called the woman out and told her she was free from whatever had caused her disability. Immediately, she was made straight, and began praising God! It doesn't matter what you are struggling with, or how long you've been struggling with it … you can be healed.

The strange thing is, Jesus didn't ask her what she needed or if she wanted to be healed, which is what He was known for. She didn't have to say a word. This tells me that sometimes your healing may be in simply showing up. Not only was the woman healed physically; her spirit was healed also. If you are in need of something, love yourself enough to go where help is.

If you are in need of something, love yourself enough to go where help is.

Self-Love

According to the *American Heritage Dictionary*, self-love is "the instinct or desire to promote one's own well-being; regard for or love of one's self." If you have always provided for other people in some way, you are, more than likely, one of those people who feels guilty loving on yourself. I believe many people struggle with practicing self-love because it can look and feel selfish. You need to know that selfishness and self-centeredness is very different from self-love. When a person is selfish and self-centered, they care for themselves ONLY! Their primary concern is their own needs and interests, regardless of anyone else's. A selfish person expects to benefit in EVERY situation. Self-love is simply taking care of yourself, making sure you are O.K. physically, mentally, spiritually and emotionally.

Self-love means something different for each of us. The way you love yourself is completely dependent on what you deem as love. However, the most important thing is that you do it. LOVE YOURSELF! If you don't love yourself, you'll accept any kind of treatment. The more you love and care for yourself, the easier it will be to determine or identify what's good for you and what's not.

Be Honest About Where You Are

Helping others is an act of kindness. It shows humility and good noble character. However, many of us take it to the extreme. We completely neglect ourselves while giving all our attention to everything and everyone else. I have found that when you live in a constant state of sacrifice, you live an unhealthy, energy- drained life. Your personal needs are valid, and disregarding them could be detrimental. Unfortunately, many people have suffered the consequences … which is the reason I wrote this book!

How many times have you responded, "I'm fine" when asked, "How are you?" The truth is, you have a million and one things going on. You feel hurt, sad, depressed, frustrated, aggravated, disgusted, dropped, abandoned, misunderstood, rejected, overwhelmed, lost, empty, used, confused, distressed, wounded, ashamed, condemned, judged, beaten, and broken. These emotions are real. You could be experiencing some of them right now. Don't go through life acting as if they don't exist – you're setting yourself up for disaster. Ignoring these feelings will only ensure continued pain and suffering. Acknowledge where you are. Be considerate of your feelings, and give yourself permission to take care of *you.*

While you're getting used to loving and nurturing yourself, don't make the mistake of rejecting love from someone else. A huge part of loving yourself is being able to accept love from others. Most importantly, allow yourself to be used and loved by God. There is no greater love than His: *"There is no greater love than to lay down one's life for one's friends"* (John 15:13, NLT).

Confronting the Inner Critic

The cruelest remarks you'll ever hear come from the inner critic. Your inner critic is always at work, trying to convince you that you're not good enough. It robs you of your self-confidence and causes you to second-guess or run away from your purpose. When you don't operate in your purpose, you never accomplish your God-given assignment. We all have an inner critic that expresses criticism, disapproval, and judgement.

Here are some of the things your inner critic might say:

"What's wrong with you?"

"Why didn't you … ?"

"You're not intelligent enough."

"You should be further along."

Not only does your inner critic use guilt-inducing comments to manipulate your behavior; other people will use them as well. They think that if you feel bad enough about yourself, your actions will change. Understand that the critic's goal is to control you, your thoughts and your conduct. Over time, the persistent negative self-talk causes you to become stuck.

Many people never deal with their inner critic. They either believe it, or avoid it. Some keep busy to stay out of their own heads. The problem with avoidance is that it can cause you to develop addictive behaviors … promiscuity, drinking or smoking, just to name a few. After you engage in these things for so long, they'll become what you use to soothe the pain inside you.

Ultimately, you'll experience shame. Shame makes you go inside yourself and keeps you withdrawn from others. It's another one of satan's tactics to keep us disconnected from one another. You tend to isolate yourself when you feel flawed. You are embarrassed around people, because it seems like a spotlight is shining on your inadequacies. When someone gives you a compliment, your inner critic tells you it's a lie. It's not easy to stand up to yourself. The one thing you need to confront your inner critic is usually the first thing attacked, and that's your boldness and courage.

To successfully confront the voice within, you need to be aware that you have one. Many of us don't even realize its presence. Pay attention to the first thought that comes to mind during the highs and lows of your life. What do you think about yourself? Who are you comparing yourself to, and why? To get a clear understanding of where these thoughts are coming from, you must really dig deep within yourself and search for the most vulnerable feelings you have about the situation you're facing. Ask yourself these questions:

1. **What am I afraid of?**

2. **Why am I doubting myself?**

3. **Why do I believe these thoughts?**

Your critical inner voice increases feelings of self-hatred, and if you're not careful, it eventually causes you to turn on yourself. The inner critic can ruin your life. It often drives you to make poor decisions that result in a destructive lifestyle. Have you ever noticed a sudden change in your mood for no apparent reason? Here's the reason for that. Your inner voice is usually responsible for these emotional shifts. These impulsive changes in your mood, as well as negative emotions, can be hard to manage. You have to pray consistently and surrender yourself to God, allowing Him to take control. Yes, it's true that medication can balance your hormones and improve your feelings, but pills are limited in their ability to bring true healing for the mind. Only God has the power to do that. *"Instead, let the spirit renew your thoughts and attitudes"* (Ephesians 4:23, NLT).

PRAYER
"Look Within"

Dear Lord,

Guilt and shame have overtaken me. I have so many regrets that taunt me daily. My past is not perfect, but I have comfort in knowing that You *are*.

Deliver me from the bondage of my past. Rescue me from the guilt and shame I feel from what I did as well as what others did to me. Give me a clean heart; a forgiving heart. Lord, make me over again. Don't allow bitterness to contaminate my spirit, or resentment to poison my soul. Show me how to live in the present and not in the past. Empower me to take control over my emotions and live a life of love, peace, and harmony. Amen.

- 4 -
THE SHADOW OF DEATH

Yea, though I walk through the valley of the shadow of death, I will fear no evil:

*for thou art with me; thy rod and thy staff they comfort me. (**Psalm 23:4, KJV**)*

David, the psalmist, is describing a very low place in this passage. In my opinion, this verse is the most riveting in the twenty-third Psalm. When I think of "the valley of the shadow of death," I think of the darkest, coldest, most somber place imaginable. *Clarke's Commentary on the Bible* refers to it as "the dead of the night." The Hebrew word for "shadow of death" is darkness, and the root word is "death."

When you're walking in complete darkness, you lose your sense of direction. There may be a way out, but you can't see it. It's uncomfortable because you're vulnerable; you are exposed to pitfalls. This is no place of pleasure and contentment. Rather, it is a place of sadness and grief. Sadness and grief are very real emotions that even God himself experienced. In John 11:35, Jesus wept. In Mark 3:5, Jesus was angry and grieved. In Matthew 26:37-38, He was sorrowful. Always remember that whatever you feel, Jesus probably felt it too at some point.

We live in a world where being honest about where you are (emotionally) is unpopular and sometimes forbidden. Even in the church, it's not always considered spiritual to say you're tired or overwhelmed. Some deem that type of transparency as irreverent and ungodly. The reality is that when people feel they can't be honest, they tend to lie. If you have actively participated in ministry for a long time, you have probably experienced burnout at some point. Most people keep this hidden for fear of what it looks like. No one wants to look as though they have abandoned their ministry. So, they'll let the fear of guilt be the charge that keeps them moving. When you keep going without taking a break, it's like a person who drives drunk. You're not focused, your vision is blurred, and your judgment is off. You're bound to dismantle your life, possibly even someone else's.

We should all strive to create an environment in our relationships, workplaces and ministries that welcomes honesty and openness. As strange as it may seem, some of the most powerful and influential people in the world secretly feel as though they are ineffective or useless. Take the case of the Georgia pastor who committed suicide just weeks after talking another man out of killing himself. According to the website ChristianNews.net, Teddy Parker, 41, senior pastor of Bibb Mt. Zion Baptist Church in Macon, GA, shot himself in his driveway on November 10, 2013. Parker's congregation of 800 waited for him to preach at an afternoon service for which he never showed up. According to the article, Parker's wife returned home after he failed to arrive at church – and found him dead in his car. I can only imagine the grief his family, friends and church members felt. Parker's longtime friend, Dr. E. Dewey Smith Jr., told reporters that "Parker was suffering from depression, and was in treatment, but he just couldn't step away from ministry."

> *We should all strive to create an environment in our relationships, workplaces and ministries that welcomes honesty and openness.*

Smith preached the funeral and made a powerful statement to those who gathered: "As a church member, either you're an armor bearer, or a pallbearer – helping your pastor get to his destiny, or carrying him slowly to his death."

An Exhausted Mind

Dr. Jonathan Drummond–Webb, 45, a famous pediatric heart surgeon, took his life on Christmas night in 2004. He overdosed on pain pills and alcohol. Webb was the chief heart surgeon at Arkansas Children's Hospital. He was recognized for his outstanding work in a four–part ABC News documentary in 2002. At the time, Drummond–Webb had performed 830 surgeries with a two percent mortality rate. This was the lowest mortality rate of any pediatric surgeon in the country. The hospital's chief executive officer said that Drummond–Webb worked tirelessly to save his patients.

Many people wondered how a man who devoted his life to saving so many lives could take his own. Drummond-Webb's friends said they believed he suffered from a sudden bout of depression from an extremely stressful year. According to the Dec. 27, 2004 edition of the *Arkansas Times* newspaper, the doctor had expressed anger and frustration in his suicide note. But years prior, he'd made a short statement to a reporter that far too many people took lightly. He said, "I don't get out much, and I need a break."

Although the doctor and the pastor both suffered from depression and may have had deep–rooted issues, their minds were probably exhausted. The demands on their lives literally sucked the life out of them.

Sometimes the people who say, "I need a break" don't take it seriously enough, nor do the people who hear those words spoken. I believe in this case, it was a matter of life and death. Time off is not popular among hardworking people who are passionate about what they do, but rest is required for your sanity. Your job or life may not be demanding according to the *world's* perception, but if it's stressful to *you*, that's all the reason you need to press "pause!" We have become so far removed from rest that we don't even use the word "sabbatical" anymore. It's like a foreign language. Sabbaticals are vital because they give you an opportunity to "re–up" in order to avoid burnout. They allow you to rejuvenate, refresh, refocus, recharge and recover.

According to The Francis A. Schaeffer Institute of Church Leadership Development:

70% of pastors constantly fight depression

71% of pastors are burned out

70% of pastors say ministry negatively affected their families

70% of pastors say they don't have a close friend

Rest Is Not a Sin

> **The apostles returned to Jesus from their ministry tour and told him all they had done and taught. Then Jesus said, "Let's go off by ourselves to a quiet place and rest awhile." He said this because there were so many people coming and going that Jesus and his apostles didn't even have time to eat. So they left by boat for a quiet place, where they could be alone. But many people recognized them and saw them leaving, and people from many**

> **towns ran ahead along the shore and got there ahead of them. Jesus saw the huge crowd as he stepped from the boat, and he had compassion on them because they were like sheep without a shepherd. So he began teaching them many things. (Mark 6:30-34, NLT*)*

According to *Matthew Henry's Concise Commentary on the Whole Bible*, "Christ notices the fright of some apostles, and toils of other disciples, and provides rest for those who are tired, and refuge for those that are terrified. Some were excited by their success, and needed calming down even more than physical rest. So, Jesus knowing their need, instructed them to come with him into healing solitude, and rest awhile."

The commentary also tells how "Christ came into the world, not only to restore, but to preserve, and nourish spiritual life; in Him there is enough for all that come. None are sent away from Christ empty, but the ones who are full of themselves." By now, you should understand how essential rest is, and that there is nothing ungodly or unrighteous about succumbing to it.

There are many more benefits to rest than the obvious. Rest recharges your mind. I'm sure you remember an instance where you (or someone else) said, "Let me sleep on it" before making a decision. Indeed, you can make good, sound decisions after you've gotten a little rest. You may find yourself thinking in a totally different direction.

I must remind myself of this daily, and I encourage you to remember it as well: You cannot live a well-balanced life without rest. The impact that the lack of rest has on you is always underestimated. The consequences are severe ... sometimes even deadly.

Every culture and country must deal with the problem of suicide. However, almost 40,000 Americans commit suicide each year. Depression and suicide have been issues for thousands of years.

The impact that the lack of rest has on you is always underestimated.

Suicides in The Bible

Abimelech – A woman threw a millstone at him and cracked his skull. He told his armor bearer to kill him because he didn't want anyone to say he was killed by a woman. **Judges 9:54**

Samson – He killed himself getting revenge on the Philistines. **Judges 16:30**

Saul – He was severely wounded by Philistine archers, so he told his armor bearer to kill him. His armor bearer wouldn't do it, so Saul fell on his sword. As it happened, the wound did not kill Saul immediately. So, he had an Amalekite stranger to pierce him with the sword. **1 Samuel 31:4; 2 Samuel 1:1-10**

Saul's Armor Bearer – He could not live without Saul, so he fell on his sword to kill himself. **1 Samuel 31:5**

Ahithophel – A man who was praised for his wisdom, he saw that his advice had not been followed. He went home, gave his family instructions, and hanged himself. **2 Samuel 17:23**

Zimri – He was a high-ranking military commander who killed his king and assumed the throne himself. The people of Israel elected their own king (Omri). When Zimri realized that he was a wanted man whose situation was irrecoverable, he went inside the palace of the king's house and set it on fire. **1 King 16:18-19**

Judas – He received money for betraying Jesus. He regretted what he had done, and went away to hang himself. **Matthew 27:5**

Each of these men dealt with issues that are common even today. **Abimelech** had a fear of being humiliated by a woman. He obviously had ego issues. **Samson** was bitter from being betrayed, and wanted revenge. **Saul** felt isolated, and the silence of God was too much for him. **Saul's armor bearer**'s grief, and loyalty to a dead master, caused him to commit suicide. **Ahithophel** could not handle rejection. He also felt irrelevant and ineffective. He was once respected and admired for his wisdom, but people no longer responded to his advice. **Zimri** was a rebellious traitor who was hopeless. **Judas** was full of regret.

If any of these feelings ever arise in you, you should be quick to pray and ask God to take control of your emotions before your emotions take control of you. The calamities of life have the power to destroy you, but God is in the refurbishing business! He has the power to reconstruct. He'll take what's left of you

> *God is talking even when He's silent. Sometimes, you have to stop trying to listen for Him, and start looking for Him.*

and make you new again. For those of you who feel isolated and are experiencing the "silence of God" just like Saul, or Pastor Parker in Macon, GA., know that God is talking even when He's silent. Sometimes, you have to stop trying to listen for Him, and start looking for Him. You might even encounter seasons when you can't hear *or* see Him. In those times, you must do what the song says ... "When you can't trace Him, or track Him, just **trust** Him!"

PRAYER

"The Shadow of Death"

Dear Lord,

I know that You have all power in Your hands. I'm casting all my cares upon You, and trusting in Your Word. My heart is wounded and my mind is tired. Give me comfort and strength in my darkest valley. Help me to not turn against myself. Give me the will to live. Put an end to my silent suffering. Give me the courage to admit when I'm living in torment. Stand up in me and empower me to walk in authority. Clean my heart and regulate my mind. Renew my spirit. Fill me with Your love. Lift every burden and heal every hurt. Restore my soul, and keep me in perfect peace. Amen

- 5 -
OFF BALANCE

Then Jesus said, "Come unto me, all of you who are weary, and carry heavy burdens, and I will give you rest.

(Matthew 11:28, NLT)

Several years ago, I worked for a company called Watkins Freight. They were eventually bought out by FedEx Freight. I was the logistics clerk for one of the terminals. I processed and printed the delivery/shipment sheets for all the truck drivers on the day shift. I was responsible for managing and maintaining a record of the freight on the trailer. Customers would often call in to check the arrival times of their shipments, so I would check the list as well as the location of the driver to give an ETA (estimated time of arrival).

I could only do my job effectively if the dockhands properly loaded the freight. If you've ever worked on a shipping and receiving dock, you know how important it is to load the trailer accurately. It might seem trivial, but there is an art to loading a trailer. It must be done strategically. The supervisor would constantly drill the dockhands and forklift operators on the importance of weight distribution. Improperly distributed weight in the trailer could cause a serious, even fatal accident on the road. The load has a lot to do with how well the truck operates. (I'm going somewhere with this, so stay with me, readers!) Many people in this line of work have lost their jobs due to a trucking accident caused by a trailer swinging out of control. Drivers have been killed because the load shifted and caused the tractor and trailer to turn over. Usually, a thorough post-accident investigation will reveal that the weight was not properly distributed on the trailer.

I'm sure you've seen the weigh stations that are on every major interstate in America. A weigh station is a checkpoint that requires drivers of commercial motor vehicles weighing over 10,000 pounds to pull over and drive across a scale to be weighed. These weight checks are not only for the safety of the driver, but for the roads as well – every load isn't made for every road! Some weigh stations will allow the driver to "weigh in motion" without stopping. In other cases, some drivers are required to come to a complete stop while the Department of Transportation officer conducts a safety inspection of the vehicle. The officer will check for a number of things, including flat tires, brake malfunctions, broken springs and cracked rims. Violations can result in the truck being towed and declared inoperable until repairs are complete. Not only does the officer check the weight and inspect the vehicle; he also checks the driver's log book. This is to make sure the driver has a valid license and has gotten adequate sleep as well as time off from driving.

> *Every load isn't made for every road!*

Some of you may be wondering: *What in the world do trucks and weigh stations have to do with my life being off balance?* Others can already see the picture I'm trying to paint. Don't lose focus! I'm almost finished painting.

I want to share one more important detail about weigh stations before I make the connection. Some of these stations feature scales built into the right lane of the highway about a mile ahead. When the truck rolls across the scale, a signal is sent to the transponder in the truck. A green light indicates to the driver that it's safe to keep going. If the transponder shows a red light, the driver must pull over to find out the reason for it. Failure to pull over could result in a fine or loss of driving privileges.

Over the Limit

Now here's my point. Are you driving through life carrying a load that's too heavy for you? Perhaps your load is too heavy for the road you're on (the relationship you're in). I'm sure you've heard all your life that "God won't put more on you than you can bear." Well, a lot of what's on you, God did not put there. It's clear that The Apostle Paul was writing about *temptation* in 1 Cor. 1:13. I won't go in depth regarding that passage, but I do want you to dig deep to find out what's weighing you down.

Just like a big rig, your load has a lot to do with how you function and maneuver through life. Too much weight is draining and damaging – not only for you, but the people closest to you. Sometimes it's too much of one thing that's causing you to lose ground. The control you once had over the situation is no longer there. You're unable to run this vehicle called life; instead, it's running you. What are you carrying that you need to unload?

> *Once you make the assessment, you can make the adjustments.*

To live a productive life, you *must* have balance. You must also be honest about where you are. Once you make the assessment, you can make the adjustments. Set weight limits and conduct occasional life inspections to make sure your load isn't over the limit.

The first thing you must determine: How much does your life weigh? Some loads only need readjusting, while others need to be minimized or eliminated. The quality of life is much better when your load is lighter. Heaviness will knock you off balance. It's difficult to keep your balance if you're carrying unnecessary weight. You might feel that it's working for *you*. But if you're connected to anyone (and most of us are), you should make sure it's working for *them* as well, especially if their feelings matter to you. As I stated before, every load isn't made for every road. This is the reason why state highway departments post "NO TRUCKS ALLOWED" signs in some places – they want to ensure the roads are well kept and maintained. Some business owners place these signs on their property also. Picture this: Your life, and the people attached to you, are your roads. Your load may consist of such obligations as work, school, or ministry. It may also include some negative situations or feelings, such as family drama, anxiety, infidelity, debt, lying, guilt, unforgiveness, bitterness, resentment, anger and frustration.

Look at the contents of your load, and ask yourself these questions:

Is this safe?

Is there room in my life for these things?

Are my loved ones strong enough to handle this?

Is my load causing hurt or harm to myself and others?

You don't ever want to destroy your roads, because the cost to repair them is too great. If your life is off balance and you're carrying a load that's over your limit, the best thing you can do is be open and honest about where you are. The worst thing you can do is deny your reality. One of the most dangerous conditions to develop is a condition I call "Drunk

Man Syndrome." It's a condition in which you're stumbling, staggering, and about to fall over, but in your mind, you're walking straight.

A few examples of Drunk Man Syndrome:

- **You think your marriage is solid, but it's falling apart and your spouse is miserable.**

- **You feel you have a handle on your children. In reality, they're out of control, living destructive lives.**

- **You believe your heart is pure, but your actions show that you're harboring hate and malice.**

The signs are there. Don't ignore them! Just as the driver of a commercial vehicle receives transponder signals to tell him or her whether to pull over, we have transponders in life that alert us. However, many bypass the signs, refuse to check their loads, and suffer the consequences later.

There is just as much value in rest as there is in work.

In some cases, it's not the load but rather the *driver* who needs a readjustment. Maybe all you need is sleep. When you have not had adequate rest, your judgment is off. You say and do things that will hurt yourself and others. Pay attention to the transponders in your life as well. Know when you've gone as far as you can go without a break. You might be the type of person who resists taking breaks. Keep in mind that there is just as much value in rest as there is in work.

I'm not saying you need to separate from your spouse or partner. I'm simply saying that you should do just as the highway driver should do ... **PULL OVER, STOP, ASSESS, and REGROUP.** To continue moving when all the warning signs are telling you to stop is dangerous and only makes matters worse. You're surely asking for a disaster. Be wise and realistic when it comes to the load you carry. Although many issues are placed upon us, most of what we carry are issues we've placed upon ourselves.

Properly distributing your weight is far from easy, especially when it seems to be out of your control. It takes daily prayer to consistently live a balanced life. For me, it took prayer *and* fasting. I want to take in "healthy portions" of family time, work, ministry, exercise and alone time.

Living a well-balanced life takes a lot of thought and intention, but it's worth it. Not only will you appreciate the benefits; everyone who loves you will appreciate them also.

PRAYER

"Off Balance"

Dear Lord,

Give me the wisdom to know when I'm over my limit. Help me to not ignore the warning signs; let me know when it's time to pull over. Teach me how to *work*, not *overwork*. Show me how to give in one area without neglecting another. I want to be well-balanced and productive. Help me to be considerate of others as well as myself. Reinforce my roads. Make them stronger until the load gets lighter. Preserve my family, preserve my life, and preserve me. Most of all, give me more of You, Lord, and less of everything else. Amen.

– 6 –
Fragile: Handle with Care

Don't look out only for your own interests, but take an interest in others, too.

(Philippians 2:4, NLT)

The LORD is close to the brokenhearted and saves those who are crushed in spirit.

(Psalm 34:18, NIV)

When a person's heart is crushed, their heart has been shattered into fragments. They're beyond wounded – they are broken. If that person is you, here's what I want you to know: Heaven rushes to restore you, and God stays close to you.

Consoling the Crushed in Spirit

As Christians, we should look for opportunities to rescue the brokenhearted, who are so often left feeling isolated and trapped in their pain.

I remember an occasion when such an opportunity presented itself to me. It was a cold Sunday evening in December. I was working on a canvas for a customer, and I realized I had run out of the paint color I needed to finish the piece. I decided to head out to Michaels (the arts and crafts store), along with my son Sirrod and daughter Anijah. When we arrived at the shopping center, Sirrod went into another store while Anijah and I went inside Michaels to look for the paint. While looking for the paint, I noticed a woman walking up with a man as well as a girl who was apparently her daughter.

The girl looked like she was my daughter's age, 17. She appeared to be extremely timid and shy. There was this uncomfortable nervousness about her that grabbed my attention immediately. I could feel that something wasn't right. The girl's body language was disturbing. I soon found out why: Out of nowhere, her mom began to scream profanities at her. Her words were gut-wrenching! The woman repeatedly called the girl a stupid idiot, and dropped the "F" bomb too many times to count. Other customers stopped and looked in total disbelief. I had never heard a mother talk to her child this way, and I found myself sad and furious at the same time.

Apparently, the daughter needed supplies for a school project, and the mother was angry that her daughter couldn't find what she was looking for. However, it was obvious that the mother had deep-rooted issues that had nothing to do with supplies: This woman was just plain evil! I felt as though I was staring satan in the face.

The girl started walking away from her mother with a look of shame and humiliation. The mother then looked at the man who was with them and said, "She's walking away because she's f-ing embarrassed." At this point, I'm thinking, *Wouldn't you be embarrassed?* It took everything in me to not jump to this young girl's defense. She was so hurt and helpless, and that made me feel very bad for her. I wondered why the man with them never said anything. He seemed to be just as scared as the girl. Apparently, he knew to keep his mouth shut!

I kept saying to myself, *This is awful! God, please give me a chance to comfort this young girl.*

After telling her daughter to go find the "f-ing" supplies, the mother stormed off. The daughter began to walk to a back corner of the store. I knew this was my opportunity to "console the crushed in spirit." I *had* to find this girl to encourage her, I told Anijah.

We walked to the back of the store, where we saw the girl covering her face. As I got closer to her, I noticed that she was crying uncontrollably. She made every attempt to hide her tears, but it was obvious what was going on. My heart ached so bad for her. I told her I'd witnessed what happened and I asked if I could give her a hug. She nodded her head while the tears continued to fall. I told her I was sorry for what happened to her and that no one deserved to be treated that way. I assured her that God loved her and told her that situations like this cause God to run to us. I spoke peace and blessings over her life and let her know that I would pray for her always.

After I gave her another hug, I walked away regretfully. I did not want to leave her with this woman. I was so concerned about her emotional well-being. If her mother treated her that way in a crowded store, I could only imagine what went on inside their home. I left the store that night asking God to cover the girl. My prayer was that God would heal, strengthen and protect her, then turn her situation around **suddenly!** That day is long gone, but I still think of her.

The Letter

The incident at Michaels would have bothered me on any day, but because of what had taken place the day before, it shook me up even more.

I had been researching material to get a good look at depression and its causes. I read hundreds of actual suicide notes. All of them were painful to read, but there was one I'll never forget. It was written by a sixteen-year-old girl who'd taken her life. Prepare yourself. Here's how the letter read.

Cancelled

Mom,

If you're reading this letter, you have already found me. Consider this a gift from me. Hopefully your life will be much better now. At least you won't be sick every day. I could tell by the look on your face that I made you sick every time I walked in the room. Maybe now you can actually have a good time with your friends instead of talking about how much of a disappointment I am. I think this was the best decision for both of us. You no longer have to feel embarrassed and humiliated, and neither do I. I would much rather be dead (for real) than to walk around every day feeling worthless, lifeless, and buried in my own home. I'm sure the grave is not as cold though. I thought Jim (stepdad) would have done this to himself by now. It must be hard trying to pretend to hate me, but [being] obsessed with touching me. I've always wondered how he could live with himself. Don't you go blaming him though. Blame yourself for ignoring all the signs. Did you not think it was strange that your husband was not in bed with you at night? Did you ever question him? Did you ever walk the house to find him? Oh yea, you "did" walk the house. I remember seeing the door open and close while he was on top of me sweating like an animal. It's all over now. For me at least. If you care to have a funeral for me, please don't stand over my body screaming

"I'm sorry." Instead of apologizing to me, apologize to the sweet, kind, and loving woman who's trapped inside of you that's being held hostage by your hate and rage. For once in your life, stop being so mean Mom, and LET HER OUT!

So long, Lindsey

I had to gather myself after reading that letter. This young girl's life was over; her dreams and ambitions all gone. How could a mother be so cold toward her daughter? How could a man be turned on by a child? What would make a mother turn her face away from the abuse her daughter suffered? I can't imagine how abandoned this young girl must have felt. She couldn't turn to either parent for help. She was violated by her stepfather and betrayed by her mother. In her eyes, death was much more inviting.

If you are a parent, love and protect your children. They are a gift from God, as stated in Psalm 127:3 (NLT): *"Children are a gift from the Lord; they are a reward from him."* Without the protection and covering of a parent, a child is left completely exposed and vulnerable to all kinds of injustice. Your home should not only serve as a physical shelter for them, but also a safe place that's free of emotional, mental, verbal and physical abuse. It should be a place where they can openly share their feelings and concerns without being attacked. No child should live in fear!

Watch your child's movements and mannerisms for any signs that they might be undergoing mistreatment. We all – children and adults – say a whole lot without speaking. Some children cry out by acting out, while others cry out in silence. Yes, we make mistakes as parents, but we should strive to become experts in monitoring our children's behavior.

Here are five questions to ask yourself if you suspect your child is being abused:

Have their habits changed?

What are they doing that they have never engaged in before?

What have they stopped doing that they have always done?

Are they withdrawn?

Have their grades dropped significantly?

As parents, we must be present for our children so that we can pick up on these things. I'm not speaking of being physically present only. We must be *emotionally* connected and tied to our children. Some parents are so consumed with everything else in their lives, their children get only what's left over. We live in a day and age where thirty- , forty- , and fifty-year-olds are trying to *relive* their youth instead of *raising* their youth. I believe that's why so many children are self-destructive and suffer from depression without their parents' knowledge. Children are living in homes where the parents are never there. Or they are there, but refuse to interact with their children. It's as if the parents are off-limits, like a formal sitting room. This teaches children to either reject closeness, or long for it. In other words, they'll become adults who either push everyone away or want to be close to everyone they meet.

Then there are mothers and fathers who feel that being a drill sergeant and running the house like a boot camp makes them the "model parent." Yes, children need structure and guidance, but there is more to being a parent than being a disciplinarian. Develop a relationship with your children that makes them comfortable talking to you. They won't be young always. As they grow older, you'll have to change the way you parent them, but you want that foundation to be laid. If you keep living, a day will come when you'll need or want your child's company ... but if you never welcomed it when the child was growing up, it will be next to impossible to establish a close relationship with that child later. When adults have an unfulfilling relationship with their parents, it's usually because of something that stemmed from childhood. It's hard to be emotionally close to someone who has always been emotionally distant.

God wants parents to love their children, and children to honor their parents. If you are an adult who is experiencing discord between you and a parent, open your heart. Ask God to drive out disharmony and conflict, and fill you up with His peace and love. Cancel the debt of offense. Let it go! Forgive and pray for those who failed you.

A Heart of Compassion

Can you imagine a world full of compassion? Think about it. If everyone showed compassion, there would literally be no one in need. Here's why I say that.

Having compassion means to be deeply concerned or disturbed by someone else's suffering, loss or tragedy – so much so that you want to ease their pain or even reverse the situation. Showing compassion gives a clear picture of the condition of your heart, much like an X-ray. Many people turn their faces away from the adversities and hardships of others, making comments such as "He or she should have known better," "You reap what you sow," "I disagree with the choices that they make," "God is dealing with them," or simply ignoring them altogether.

As a Christian, you should never try to determine whether a person's priorities are in order, or whether they made wise decisions, before you show compassion. If a person is in urgent need of help, there's no time to do a background check. Comments like those mentioned above are usually made to justify the commenter's lack of help and support. The worst part about it all is when people use God to make themselves feel better about turning their faces away from others' pain.

Your compassion could change the course of someone's life. **So often, we miss out on opportunities to minister to the heart of a man, focusing on the habits of the man. Keep in mind that** showing compassion does not condone the recipient's actions; it confirms your Godly attribute! You cannot claim to be a child of God and not have a heart for people. Don't be so quick to close your eyes or turn a deaf ear to someone else's calamity. No one is exempt from bad breaks, disaster, sorrow, misery or grief. There will come a time in your life when you'll be faced with some type of misfortune, and you'll need someone to be compassionate toward you.

> *Showing compassion does not condone the recipient's actions; it confirms your Godly attribute!*

Some people fail to show compassion because they are blinded by their own opinions, whereas others are blinded by their success and status. I love the song "All the Way Up" by Fat Joe and Remy Ma. It's my "get hype" workout song. It's good to be "all the way up." But don't think, just because you're all the way up, that you can't come all the way back down. Living all the way up does not work well for some. Research has shown that **when people have *more*, they care *less*.** According to ScientificAmerican.com, wealth and status decrease your feelings of compassion toward others. The article goes on to reveal how "wealth and abundance gives us a sense of freedom and independence from others" and that "the less we have to rely on others, the less we may care about their feelings."

Be mindful of others, just as Christ is mindful of you. Also, while showing kindness to others, remember to include yourself in the circle of compassion as well.

Handle with Care

I've been painting abstract art professionally for eight years. I love using a blank canvas to create a masterpiece. I'm always amazed at the finished piece of work. Some paintings take hours to complete, while others take days. Regardless of the amount of time spent on each one, they're all valuable. My paintings are like my babies. I'm emotionally attached to all of them. As I'm painting, it's as if I'm watching my children grow and blossom.

Because of the paintings' worth, and my attachment to them, I'm very protective. Whenever we moved, I made sure that whoever transported my artwork was being extremely careful with it. They had to carry the paintings a certain way and watch out for anything that could puncture or damage them. It was always hard for me to take my eyes off the paintings. I couldn't finish what I was working on because I was too busy focusing on my artwork! It usually worked out better if I just carried the paintings myself. When it came time to ship a painting to a customer, I'd make sure the box was marked "Fragile, handle with care." The packaging may not have been elaborate, but the content inside was priceless. I didn't want it tossed around carelessly or otherwise mishandled.

God feels the same way about His children, especially the ones who feel hopeless ... so much so that He stays close to those who are brokenhearted: *"The Lord is close to the brokenhearted; he rescues those whose spirits are crushed"* (Psalm 34:18, NLT).

Just as Jesus cares for those who are in distress, we should also. Many people turn their faces from others who are in need or hurting. People who are depressed or suicidal feel worthless. If you walk away from them as if they don't matter, you only contribute to their feelings of insignificance. In their minds, your actions support their belief.

Every day, you should strive to make a positive impact on someone's life. You never know how close a person is to throwing it all away. Some people are far beyond fragile; they're shattered. That means their heart and mind are in pieces along with their broken spirit. They're emotionally all over the place. Something, or someone, has dismantled them.

As you go throughout life, showing compassion should always be on your agenda.

There are enough people in the world doing well that no one should be hungry or hurting. It grieves my heart to see people who live lavishly while watching others suffer, emotionally or financially, right under their noses. If you have the resources, *help them.* Even if you feel as though you have nothing to offer, search yourself to see how you can help. I believe each of us has something that someone needs.

Again, don't wait to determine whether a person deserves help. Respond to the immediate need and find out the back story later. It confuses me when people require more out of others than Jesus does! It's as if they have placed themselves above God, which is a dangerous place to be. Be careful how you treat those who are less fortunate than you. Remember, your money and status does not cover and keep you; God's grace does. If He decides to withdraw His grace from you, you might find yourself living among those you once ignored: *"Whoever gives to the poor will lack nothing, but those who close their eyes to poverty will be cursed."* (Proverbs 28:27, NLT)

I remember a cold day in February when I was headed to a public storage facility to help a friend store some belongings. When I pulled up, I noticed a man who was about 6 feet, four inches tall, standing near the building with a huge bag. When I got out of the car I spoke to him, and he politely spoke back. I walked in the building and realized I had left my cellphone in the car, so I ran back out to get it. Just as I was walking back inside the storage facility, the man standing outside asked if he could help. The woman at the front desk heard him and said, "Ma'am, we don't typically deal with *them.*"

"What do you mean?" I asked. "Because I typically *do.*"

"Those people hang around here, and all they do is beg," she replied. She had a look of disgust on her face that would keep anyone away.

I didn't want the man to see or hear her, so I stepped outside to talk to him. I asked him how much he would charge to help us unload the U-Haul truck.

"Whatever you give me is fine; anything helps," he said.

I told him to give us a few minutes to get the paperwork finished up, and then I'd let him know when we were ready.

That paperwork seemed to take forever. *Since when did it take so long to rent a storage unit?* I wondered. I also wondered whether the woman who worked there was moving slow, hoping the man would leave. (Some people have a problem with others getting their needs met, even if they are not the ones meeting the needs!)

The man stood at the corner of the building, waiting patiently. We finally finished up, and I went outside to tell him we were ready. While we were unloading the U-Haul, I found out that his name was Donnie. When I learned that he had children my age, I felt it was only right to call him *Mr.* Donnie. My mother had always told my brothers and me to "put a handle" on an adult's name, and although I'm an adult myself, he was twice my age. My respect for him did not diminish because he was homeless and needed help. The fact that he was a human being, and old enough to be my father, was enough for me to show respect.

Mr. Donnie had a warm spirit and a peculiar presence. It felt as though we were in the company of God. He made me think of Hebrew 13:2 (NLT): *"Don't forget to show hospitality to strangers, for some who have done this have entertained angels without realizing it!"*

When we finished unloading the truck, I talked to Mr. Donnie for a while to find out where he hung out. I told him I would come find him to make sure he had food. Before I left, I made sure he had enough money to buy food for the next two weeks.

I believe all people are necessary and have a purpose in life. It's the responsibility of those who are in a better a position to offer help and hope to the ones who are less fortunate. Not only can a kind word or gesture brighten someone's day; it can change that person's life. **You have to be careful to not be so consumed with your own issues that you completely disregard someone else's.** Be mindful of others. Be sensitive to those in need.

When we were back at the storage facility unloading the U-Haul, one of the employees walked by with a bag of to-go dinners. We could smell the food before she even got close to us. She walked past Mr. Donnie as if he was invisible. She was so unmoved. Some might say she didn't have to offer her lunch to him. That's true; she didn't *have* to, but she should have *wanted* to. I wondered how many times Mr. Donnie had to watch people walk by without giving him a second thought, despite his obvious need.

Mr. Donnie seemed hopeful even as a homeless man. But let's just say he was contemplating suicide, yet looking for reasons to live. What if he'd heard the woman at the front desk say, "We don't deal with them"? That statement could have been the fatal blow. I don't know if the women who worked at the storage facility were Christians or not, but those of us who are should act like it. You don't have to go around quoting Scriptures to people who may not understand the Bible, or hand out Bibles to people who may not know how to read. Let your *life* be an example to those who don't know Christ, or who are in such a dark place that they can't see Him. People should see *Christ* through *you*. Your words and your deeds should be a reflection of Him: *"In the same way, let your light shine before others, that they may see your good deed, and glorify your Father in heaven"* (Matthew 5:16, NIV).

Look for opportunities to help. When people are down to nothing, they tend to believe they have nothing to live for. Depression and suicide are more prevalent among those who are extremely oppressed. That's why it's so important to "handle them with care." Your chance to help someone might come in strange ways. Remember that everyone who needs assistance does not need money. Some people need to hear a kind word, while others need a listening ear. Whatever the case may be, make every attempt to shine your light in a dark situation. I believe God strategically places certain people and circumstances in our way to see how we will respond. I can imagine God watching and waiting to see if we will show love by building others up, or show hate by tearing them down. Everything Christ did was out of love, and God's children should not be doing anything different from that.

When I was at the storage facility, Mr. Donnie asked a question that each of us can learn from. He asked, "Can I help you?" Although he was asking because he was in need, the phrase itself is simply not used enough. We must learn to stop running away from the needs of others and run toward them. Instead of frowning, we should smile. Instead of discouraging, we should encourage. We must get to a place where we are getting a grip on those who are in pain, or at least pointing them in the right direction.

I understand that some of you might be drained from being pulled on so much. That's an issue that should be addressed as well, but that's not what I'm speaking of. There is a difference between someone pulling on you and someone who needs relief.

A lot of the poverty people experience has nothing to do with a financial need. They may have poor health (physical, emotional and/or spiritual) that causes them to suffer in every area of life. Be sensitive to those who are fragile and handle them with care. Any little thing can cause them to break. Keep in mind that many people ended their lives at their breaking point.

If you are reading this and you feel broken, just know that although your brokenness may be a problem for you, it's not a problem for God. He wants to heal you and make you whole again.

Although your brokenness may be a problem for you, it's not a problem for God.

The 2016 Olympic cycling races were incredible. There were countless life lessons in each race. A case in point: While walking past the television one day, I noticed that a car was keeping up with one cyclist. There were two men in the car. One man was driving, while the other was leaning out the back window to adjust the seat on the cyclist's bike. A bike rack was attached to the roof of the car; the cyclist held the rack with his left hand and used his right hand to guide the bike. He never stopped pedaling. He didn't have to drop out of the race, nor did he fall behind. He continued to hold on to the car until the adjustments were made to his bike. I was even more amazed to realize that before I'd started watching the race, the cyclist had apparently fallen. The man who was hanging out of the back window had been sanitizing and dressing a wound on the rider's arm!

As I stared in awe, I couldn't help but wonder what the world would be like if all of us were like that man who did everything in his power to make sure the cyclist finished the race. When you come across someone riding through life, struggling and hurting, what will your response be? That person needs *you* to serve as a pillar of strength; to say, "Keep pedaling! I've got you."

PRAYER

"Fragile: Handle With Care"

Dear Lord,

Thank You for every opportunity You've given me to show love. I confess that I haven't always responded in a way that pleases You. Forgive me for all the times I made excuses or looked away. Help me to be more sensitive to the needs of others without blame or judgement. Give me a heart of compassion; a heart that comforts those who are hurting; and a heart that's generous to those who are less fortunate. Help me to rush to those who are suffering and in distress. Lord, my desire is to love the way You do. Give me a forgiving heart that overlooks offenses – so much so that I even help those who would not help me. Teach me how to address my pain, but not get so wrapped up in my own life that I dismiss someone else's needs. Most of all, thank You for being the greatest example of compassion. Amen

− 7 −
STAND TALL

Be on guard. Stand firm in the faith. Be courageous. Be strong. And do everything with love.

(1 Corinthians 16:13-14, NLT)

A few years ago, living in Arkansas, I noticed an art gallery with beautiful fine art displayed in its front window. I drove past the gallery every day, looking for new art on display and imagining my own paintings hanging there. Many times, I considered stopping. After some months went by, I finally got up enough nerve to go inside and inquire.

This particular day I pulled up in front of the art gallery, which was next door to a busy bagel shop. The aroma of fresh bagels and coffee met me in the parking lot, but the moment I stepped inside the gallery, the overpowering scent of expensive oil paints and wooden picture frames greeted me. As I looked around, I was blown away by the detail of the paintings. My initial thought was that I was way out of my league. These artists were extremely talented. They were selling eight-inch-by-ten-inch paintings for five hundred dollars! I figured I should just turn around and leave before anyone approached me.

As I was about to do just that, a small-framed woman, who appeared to be in her late fifties, approached me. "Hello. How can I help you?" she asked. The woman had a regal presence, but her manner was warm and inviting. Encouraged by this, I told her I had been admiring the art in the gallery window for months and wanted to know how to get my work in the gallery.

The woman was very forthcoming with information. She gave me a full tour of the gallery and told me they had seventeen artists, but had room for one more. I immediately got butterflies because I knew I was going to go for it! She told me the monthly fee for artists ($150), and offered me the one spot available. I let her know that I needed to talk the matter over with my husband. I went home and talked to Jason about it. As always when I want to begin a new venture, he said, "Let's make it happen." I called and told the woman at the gallery that it was a go and that I would return the next day to finalize everything.

The next morning, I went back to the gallery and paid my first $150 to become a member. I was a bit nervous at the thought of paying this amount every month, but I'd done it – I'd stepped outside my box! Well, it was more like a *jump* outside my box. It was truly a leap of faith.

When I moved my paintings into the gallery, the woman who'd offered me the membership showed me the workroom and taught me how to professionally install wiring to hang my paintings. She gave me full access to all the tools and supplies. I'll never forget her telling me to value my work, because if I didn't, no one else would. Her input and advice were extremely helpful. I respected her even more when she informed me that she was not in her fifties but was, in fact, in her late seventies. She was an artist also, and to be honest, her work stood out among that of the other, younger artists in the gallery.

Every day I stopped by the gallery, I met a different artist. Not only was I the youngest, I was the only black artist. Many of these artists drove luxury cars and bragged about how they paid cash for them. They lived in palatial homes located along the Arkansas River, with breathtaking views of Pinnacle Mountain west of the city. Most of them had maids, housekeepers, and groundskeepers. Most of their spouses and children were doctors or heads of investment and finance Firms. Although we lived very different lives, we all had one thing in common. We were artists trying to sell our work.

Every second Friday was Art Night at the Courtyard by Marriott in downtown Little Rock, which displayed works by artists at the gallery. Each artist-member was asked to sign up to do a "live" painting (create a work onsite) at the hotel on an Art Night with the intention of selling the painting. Soon, my turn came. My live-painting event was a festive affair, complete with Jason playing keyboard. My piece sold before I even finished painting. A couple who had been sitting at the bar walked up and said, "We want it." It was a nice Art Night debut for me.

That was only the beginning. Two weeks later, a gentleman who was in town on business saw my artwork on display at the hotel and purchased two of my paintings. A week later, another businessman purchased one of my paintings. A few days later, the general manager of a nearby hotel wanted a large painting – by me – to hang in that hotel's lobby. I was amazed at the number of paintings I had sold in such a brief time! All the other artists at the gallery congratulated me. They appeared to be supportive.

But then, it happened. The masks came off! The next thing I knew, the same people who had been so friendly and talkative at first were hardly speaking. When customers visited the gallery, they were told I was no longer a member. I was contacted by the chairman of an art show I attend every year; he asked if I would be attending that particular year because he had received a phone call informing him that I would not be attending the show. He went on to say that he found that hard to believe, considering how well I had done at the show the previous year. I tried to get him to tell me who'd contacted him and given my regrets, but he claimed not to recall the person's identity.

Cancelled

Then there was the day I attended an impromptu meeting at the gallery. The meeting was ostensibly to discuss marketing strategies, but to my surprise, it was an ambush. The once sweet, poised, and soft-spoken woman who'd taken me in as a member expressed frustration about the amount of art supplies and hardware that were being used ... the same items she'd given me full access to when I first became a member. She and a few of the others complained about how much the hardware cost, so a new rule was implemented: Each time it was used, a percentage would be added to the monthly member fee. Paying for the hardware was not a problem. The issue for me was that the other artists had never been required to pay for supplies before. One artist, in fact, said, "This must be something new. I had never heard of this before."

I knew this had nothing to do with hardware and supplies, but everything to do with the fact that I had become the top seller in the gallery. I left the meeting disappointed and confused. I felt my judgement had been off ... this woman had completely taken me by surprise. I also was certain that the negative energy I was now encountering would be too much to tolerate. So, I cancelled my membership and walked away from the gallery with the same class and dignity that I'd walked in with.

What I learned from this experience was life changing: Some people connected to you are O.K. with you as long as you're not producing! In their minds, you will never reach, or go beyond, their level. You're the underdog and the weakest link, and that's the position they want you to

Some people connected to you are O.K. with you as long as you're not producing!

keep. But when you tap into who you are, you begin to thrive, and when you thrive, you become a threat.

You see, I didn't have an art degree; in fact, I'd had no formal art training. The people at the gallery used my lack of knowledge and experience to feed their sense of superiority and feel like they were showing "charity." I messed that up for them! They began to see me as a threat. People who feel threatened are extremely uncomfortable. Oftentimes, they will knock you down and walk all over you in order to raise their level of comfort. When this happens, get up, dress your wounds, and with bravery and boldness, STAND TALL!

Some people, as well as some situations, are allowed into your life by God for a reason. The purpose is not always to expose the true character of others, but to make you aware of who *you* are. Without this experience, I wouldn't know how strong, creative and valuable I am. I believe God used this situation to push me past my comfort zone, past what was familiar. He was provoking me to change. I needed to be challenged, but I also needed reassurance of how much I meant to Him. I left the art gallery knowing that my gift was special, and so was I. **Although I was disappointed with what I learned about** *people*, **I'm grateful and amazed at what I learned about**

God. The way God chooses to get a message across may not be pleasurable; in fact, it might be painful. However, it's always profitable.

Boosting Your Self-Confidence

How often do negative thoughts about yourself cross your mind? I've listed 10 Scriptures to offer comfort and clarity for the negative remarks we so often make about ourselves.

1. **"I always come up short."** Romans 3:23
2. **"I have nothing of value or worth."** Matthew 10:31
3. **"God is so disappointed in me."** Romans 8:1
4. **"I'm lacking."** Ephesians 3:20
5. **"I'll never be enough."** Ephesians 2:10
6. **"I'm a failure."** Micah 7:8
7. **"I'll always be this way."** 2 Cor. 5:17
8. **"There's no hope for me."** Isaiah 43:25
9. **"It's too late for me to change."** 1 John 1:9
10. **"God made a mistake when He made me."** Isaiah 43:7

SEVEN AFFIRMATIONS FOR EVERY DAY OF THE WEEK

SUNDAY – I am thankful for my life; it has meaning and purpose. I am special and unique. There is no one on earth exactly like me. **Deut. 7:6**

MONDAY – I am chosen. I am confident. I feel good about myself. **Eph. 1:4**

TUESDAY – I am happy with the way God made me. I appreciate my unique qualities. **Gen. 1:27**

WEDNESDAY – God sees the good in me. I'm grateful to be me. **Gen. 1:31**

THURSDAY – God has called me out of darkness into His marvelous light.

I am called to be a light of the world. **1 Peter 2:9**

FRIDAY – I am fearfully and wonderfully made. I was born to succeed.

Psalms 139:14

SATURDAY – I am loved just the way I am. I am thankful that my life is full of blessings and favor. **Jeremiah 31:3**

PRAYER
"Stand Tall"

Dear Lord,

Thank You for the confidence You have given me, and for making me stronger every day. Help me to stand tall against the enemy, even if the enemy is me. Replace my negative thoughts with peace and comfort. Show me how to be strong and courageous as well as gentle and considerate of others. I pray that as You build me up, I can offer that same encouragement to someone else. Life has torn me apart, but today, I open my heart to You.

Lord, I pray that You would reconstruct every part of me, and restore me completely. Amen

– 8 –
SEEK SOLITUDE

My soul, be quiet before God, for from him comes hope.

(Psalm 62:5, ISV)

Are you experiencing a case of sensory overload? Give your mind a break. Get by yourself and learn to enjoy your own company.

Many people have different views on solitude. Some think it's the same as loneliness. It's not. "Loneliness is marked by a sense of isolation," according to an article, "Solitude vs. Loneliness," at Psychologytoday.com. "Solitude, on the other hand, is the state of being alone without being lonely, and can lead to self– awareness." I believe the difference is in your attitude toward yourself, and whether you consider "alone" time to be peaceful or dreadful.

The more you spend time with yourself, the more comfortable you'll feel being alone. The sense of freedom that comes along with solitude is incredible. It allows you to release that part of yourself that feels the need to respond to other people. We can become so obsessed with staying connected to the outside that we disregard connecting with our inner selves.

I run my businesses on social media, so it's imperative that I stay present and visible. At the same time, I have to make sure my businesses don't consume so much of me that I neglect the people and things that matter the most to me. It's in your solitude that you can gain a new perspective on every area of life. It gives you an opportunity to shape and adjust your life accordingly. You'll see your relationships, career and future with a new set of eyes. Things that used to bother you will no longer matter, and you will begin to appreciate those valuable things you may have ignored in the past.

If words like "silence" and "serenity" make you cringe, you need to ask yourself these questions:

- **Why do I fear being alone?**

- **What is it that makes me reject quietness?**

There is nothing like spending time reconnecting with yourself. We spend our whole lives getting to know everyone else, and never take time to get to know ourselves! Spending time alone can make difficult relationships a lot less frustrating; it also helps you communicate with your loved ones better. It's impossible to explain to someone else what's going on with you internally if you have no idea yourself. Solitude gives you the privacy you need to process your thoughts and feelings without distraction.

Most of the clarity I received regarding certain situations came during the times I spent with God in a quiet place. However, this has not always been the case for me.

I have four beautiful children. Whereas I was blessed with Josiah and Janiah when I married their dad, Jason, I gave birth to Sirrod and Anijah. When these two were younger, I would feel an overwhelming amount of guilt at the mere thought of being away, even for a few hours. It hasn't always been easy, but I've always loved being a mother. I love it so much that even after nineteen years, I can count the times my children and I have been apart. To this day, we enjoy each other's company.

I did whatever was necessary to create a peaceful and pleasant home for my children, even when I was in the midst of chaos that was a source of much pain. I went through a divorce that was not civil, to say the least, and spent years cleaning up debris from the wreckage. I experienced financial hardship, anger, frustration, shame, and emotional distress. Suppressing the pain I felt was no easy task. Sirrod and Anijah were both very inquisitive. They paid attention to everything. They were only two and three years old when they began noticing my watery eyes. Three-year old Sirrod would ask, "Why you trying, Mama?" – his pronunciation of "crying." (Although the word "trying" was not what he meant to say, it was in order. He had asked the million-dollar question.) Anijah would ask questions as well, but her way of comforting me was to offer me things – her toys, dolls, etc. Because they were so observant, it became very difficult to hide my emotions around them.

I was nineteen when I became a mother, but even at that early age, I was determined to be "all in." I wanted to be the best mother I could be. So, I devoted my life to God and ministry. Whenever I had to be at church, my children were there … 10:45 a.m. Sunday service, Tuesday choir rehearsal, Wednesday night Bible study, revivals, and evening programs at other churches. The church was bursting at the seams, so a 7:45 a.m. service was added. Every Sunday, I got up and made sure Sirrod and Anijah were dressed and ready for both services. There were no other options. This is how I wanted to raise my children … in church. Even when hell broke out in my home, I kept moving without ever stopping. I never fell into the cycle of dropping my children off with someone, nor did I look for opportunities to spend time alone.

My children were not a burden, but some of my life's circumstances were. There were many days I didn't want to open my eyes, let alone get out of bed. I would hear their voices and the pitter-patter of their little feet, and that was all the motivation I needed to get up and get moving.

I was a hairstylist for many years, so Sirrod and Anijah spent many days in the salon with me. They didn't spend more than a week in day care their entire lives. Since I was self-employed and had a flexible schedule, I could participate in school functions. I never missed an awards assembly. I went on every field trip. Sirrod played football for six years, and I missed only one game. Because I was so committed to being "all in," I never really considered time alone. In retrospect, I realize that I took on a lot for a young mother.

It wasn't until 2012 that I really began to embrace solitude. By this time, Jason and I had been married for two years. We were living in Maumelle, AR, when I realized how sweet the sound of silence was. I had a lightbulb come on, or an "aha" moment, as Oprah Winfrey would say. After all these years, I discovered something: Just because you don't want a break, doesn't mean you don't need one. I never realized how noisy my life had been.

Just because you don't want a break, doesn't mean you don't need one.

I love the beauty of nature. Before this point in my life, I'd never gotten a chance to take it all in and really appreciate it. We lived within walking distance of Lake Willastein. It became my favorite place in Maumelle. I would take long walks around the lake, or sit and watch the stillness of the water. It was so peaceful that it was as if the rest of the world was asleep. I didn't talk; nor did I get on my cell phone to text or scroll down my social-media newsfeed. I took pleasure in turning down the noise of life. On the days that God's voice seemed to be mixed in with everyone else's, I would walk to the lake; during these times, His voice became so much clearer. It felt as though God was saying, "I've been waiting on you, Lisha."

In the past, the enemy had used someone to make me feel guilty about all the things I could not provide for my children. It was at Lake Willastein where God reminded me of all the time I had invested in them, and assured me that nothing tangible could ever compare to my presence. I love how God uses our memories to prove His point! From then on, I looked forward to hearing from Him during my alone time.

You may be in a quiet house, but it's still loud. It's because you're surrounded by all the things that remind you of your responsibilities. When you're alone, you have the chance to think through your problems without interruption. You can reflect on your dreams, goals and life as a whole. You may not believe you need periods of solitude, but it's essential to restoring your body and conditioning your mind.

Can you remember the last time you experienced solitude? I don't mean a trip to the nail shop or the bar. I'm talking about "me time" ... total seclusion. Many people spend most of their time taking care of their families and hanging out with friends without ever connecting with themselves. This was me for many years.

I encourage you to make time for you and God. The next time you plan a girls' trip, or weekend getaway with the fellas, be sure to pencil in some alone time on your calendar as well. I never knew how much I would appreciate quietness. Not only do I seek solitude, I long for it. Like the deer pants for water, I'm desperate for God and my time alone with Him. The more you spend time with God, the more you'll find yourself craving His presence.

If your life is hectic and you can't seem to find time alone, move some things around. Readjust. Solitude is a gift from God, so satan will use anything and anyone to keep you from getting to a place where you can hear God clearly. He knows that if you could ever "quiet your mind," you will gain insight that will change the course of your life. Love your family and friends. Be excited about what you've accomplished. But don't latch on to people and things. If you do, you'll end up making your peace dependent on them. No person, no external circumstance, should determine whether you live a life of peace. **When you attach yourself to people and things with the intent to make them responsible for your peace and happiness, the spirit of loneliness will attach itself to you when they are no longer around.** When you develop a desire to spend quality time in your own presence, you enter a place of wellness ... a place that calms your mind and offers nourishment for your spirit.

I understand that solitude might be frightening for some of you. In solitude, you become familiar with who you really are. Meeting yourself might feel like meeting a stranger! Push past fear and do whatever is necessary to get in tune with yourself. Your mind can be very loud, especially if you are battling depression and thoughts of suicide. It becomes nearly impossible to hear God in noise and restlessness. If this is you, find solitude. I don't care what you have to sacrifice to get to that place; just get there. Your life depends on it!

PRAYER

"Seek Solitude"

Dear Lord,

Thank You for keeping me in the midst of chaos. When storms are raging in my life, thank You for being my peace. Show me how to balance my life and to be mindful of the time I give away. As I honor commitments to others, help me to first honor You. Open my eyes and ears to hear and see what You are revealing to me. Pour into me all that I've poured out, and fill my soul with peace. Give me a new outlook on life. Teach me how to embrace solitude and live every day of my life in Your presence. Amen

– 9 –
SWIM AWAY

My child, don't lose sight of common sense and discernment. Hang on to them, for they will refresh your soul. They are like jewels on a necklace.

(Proverbs 3:21-22, NLT)

Have you ever helped someone through their issues, only to see yours get worse? It was not just you.

As humans, we all have our issues, the most common of which are marital, relational, parental and financial. We are often drawn to try to comfort, or counsel, friends or loved ones who are suffering from their issues. Unfair as it seems, we sometimes go on to fall prey to the same issue ... and, sometimes, face even unhappier outcomes. For instance, one person might talk another through tough marital problems only to find himself or herself headed to divorce court later. The devastation can be mind boggling.

If this has happened to you, you must understand that we are the hands and feet of Jesus. He uses each of us to carry out His plan. When you save someone's child from destruction, offer tools to help free someone from financial bondage or have a hand in saving a marriage, God is glorified. On the contrary, the enemy is angry about having lost another soul, another debt prisoner, another relationship. He's furious that he couldn't destroy someone else's house, so his goal is then to catch you off guard and disrupt *yours*. In these times, you need a "spotter," a person to spot you when you're lifting the weights of life. You need a person you can trust who will cover you while you're covering someone else.

There will be times when the love you need to show won't look or feel so loving. You may have to show tough love, or maybe even walk away from a situation so that it will get better. Sometimes you must stop talking so that the person who needs help can hear from heaven. Although you mean well, your friend or loved one needs to be able to make a clear-cut distinction between your voice and God's. It really is O.K. to be quiet, listen and pray. As I indicated in the previous chapter, some of the best lessons learned were taught in silence.

Some of the best lessons learned were taught in silence.

Walking – or as I call it here, swimming – away isn't always an easy thing to do. But if you really love someone, you want them to live a better life regardless of the inconvenience it causes you or them.

Letting Go

Many years ago, I went swimming with a friend in her neighborhood pool. This friend had told me she'd learned to swim as a toddler and had loved it ever since. We had just gotten in the pool and were acclimating ourselves to the water temperature. We held on to the pool's edge as we swung our bodies toward the deep end, and remarked on how ridiculous we must look in the chilly water. Laughing uncontrollably, my friend stepped away from the edge of the pool and became frantic when she realized her feet couldn't touch the bottom. I kept screaming to her, "Just swim!" I couldn't understand why she wouldn't. Instead, she fought the water like a person who had never swum before. I grabbed her arm and tried to pull her toward the edge of the pool, but the more I pulled, the more she fought me. She kicked, swung, and dug her nails into my skin. We were both sinking, and I had to do something FAST! I was forced to go under the water, pry her hands off me and do the unthinkable: swim away. I rushed to the edge of the pool, jumped out, ran to the gate where the rescue tube was hanging, quickly snatched it off and, with all my strength, threw it in the pool. The tube landed right in front of my friend, who was still struggling to stay above water. I could tell she was getting weak, but she managed to wrap her arms tightly around the tube. I pulled her to the edge with the rope attached to the tube. It felt as though I was pulling a train.

Afterward, I couldn't believe what had just taken place. I regretted leaving my friend in the pool, but the only way to save us both was for me to swim away. She admitted that she had lied about being able to swim, and she apologized. Why did she lie? She wanted to do some of the things I could do, she said. She felt like I was good at everything and that she couldn't compare.

Seek God

Some people in your life will find themselves in trouble, and they'll start to pull on you to keep from going under. Not only can this be draining; it can be dangerous. If you're not careful, "their" struggle will cause you to sink right along with them! Sometimes you have to get yourself out of danger first in order to save someone else … in other words, you must be wise enough to know when it's time to swim away and throw in the rescue tube. In some cases, the rescue tube (God) is just the amount of space you need to put between you and the problem. So, before trying to help someone dealing with a problem, ask God for wisdom and direction. This person could be suffering with insecurities or deeply imbedded issues you know nothing about. In the case of my friend, I never knew that my abilities made her feel incompetent to the point that she would rather risk her life (and mine!) than tell the truth.

Cancelled

An elderly friend – a woman I've known all my life, and who I admire and respect – once told me a story about her past that I'll never forget. A friend she had not seen or spoken to in years reached out to her. The friend called every day with a new problem, pouring out her issues, complaining about her life and the people in it. The two women talked daily. Most times, the friend would cry throughout the entire conversation. Because my friend was genuinely concerned about this woman, she made herself available through every meltdown she had, encouraging her for hours. She prayed for her constantly, but could not stop worrying about her. The friend couldn't sleep at night; eventually my friend became irritable and restless. She kept hearing God say, "Give it to Me," but she continued to try to be there for her friend.

As time went on, my friend realized that her friend believed the world was against her. She was suspicious of everyone and everything. Finally, she became suspicious of my friend, too, and made irrational comments that only an unstable person would make. My friend racked her brain trying to figure out what had gone wrong. Again, she heard God's voice telling her to "let it go and give it to Me." This time, she did just that. And a peace came over her like never before.

In sharing her story, my friend told me to always seek God when someone pulls on me, even if it seems like a situation I can handle. The request for your attention may not be from a friend who's trying to reconnect with you; it may be a sick spirit trying to attach itself to you, she explained.

After hearing my friend's story, I'm convinced that satan has set up residence in the minds of many people. Your intentions may be pure, but a person with a diseased mind does not understand that. You cannot help a person who does not trust you. They'll never receive it. The spirit of suspicion won't allow them to do so. Be mature enough to know when the problem is too big for you. Always seek God first, and point others in His direction.

PRAYER

"Swim Away"

Dear Lord,

Thank You for giving me a heart that's drawn to those who suffer. My desire is to love the way You do. Give me Godly wisdom and discernment to know what's good for me, and what's not. Reveal to me the things the enemy tries to conceal. When someone needs me, tell me what to say and show me what to do.

I want to rely on You completely. Help me not to be overtaken by the pulling of others. Protect me from foul and unpleasant spirits. Teach me to always seek You first, and operate in Your will. Amen

– 10 –
When the Wounds Won't Heal

He heals the brokenhearted and bandages their wounds.

(Psalm 147:3, NLT)

The wounds of a person who has diabetes may be more difficult to heal than those who don't suffer from this disease. Reasons include poor blood flow to the wound, lost sensation due to nerve damage, and poorly managed wounds.

You may not be diabetic, but you could be carrying a deep wound from the past that has not healed. Whether it's recent, whether it happened at an early stage in our adulthood, or whether it's from our childhood, each of us has sustained some type of emotional wound. It might be a single incident or a cluster of events; whatever the case may be, the pain from the wound is still there. Years may have gone by, but the wound could be just as painful as it was when fresh … it could even be getting progressively worse without your even realizing it.

Since you can't see the damage the wound is causing, it might not seem so bad. But a deep wound is *always* bad. Initially it begins to decay, then it starts to rot. Once it has become rotten, not only will you be aware of the wound's continued existence; everyone else will be aware of it.

Sometimes, all it takes is a look on someone's face to trigger your pain and set you off. For instance, you may have been in a relationship with someone who didn't actually *say* "I hate you," "You make me miserable" or I wish you weren't here," but whose face took on a look of disgust whenever you entered the room. When you have been connected to a person who communicates in nonverbal ways, a look means more to you than it does to most people … and it wounds you just as much as words would. If someone else looks at you that way today, it's a painful reminder of the wound you suffered in the past.

On the other hand, someone might *have* used words to hurt you. I'm referring not just to words like "You make me sick" or "You get on my nerves." I'm talking about words that demean, devalue, and hurt you so bad that they cause physical pain. We've all heard the saying, "Sticks and stones may break my bones, but words will never hurt me." That's a lie! Words *do* hurt. Words are so powerful, they can cause you to see yourself differently. That's why the Bible tells us that *"the tongue can bring death or life"* (Proverbs 18:21a, NLT). Words can be lethal, and they don't have to be yelled or screamed. They can be spoken softly and still have the same negative effect as words spoken loudly. Words end relationships. Many people left their marriages because of what their spouses *said* to them. Even if there were actions to support the words, it's usually the words that are remembered the most. This is especially true with words conveying rejection, such as "I don't want to be here anymore" or "I want you to leave."

Some words you will never recover from without the healing power of Christ. You may have been told as a child that you were dumb and stupid, so you spent your entire life believing you were worthless. Maybe someone called you ugly or consistently pointed out your flaws. That wound is the reason you struggle with insecurities and compare yourself to others. Far too often, we make light of our wounds and the effects they have on us. We'll say, "my feelings are just hurt." The reality is that verbal abuse is killing us inside.

Have you ever been *so* hurt that you were sure you felt your heart break? I do. I remember grabbing my chest, trying to rub the pain away. The pain was so deep, I couldn't reach it. That's a different kind of pain. A pain that makes your heart ache, but causes you to feel paralyzed at the same time.

> *Just because it started off minor doesn't mean it won't escalate to something major.*

I know it hurts to give attention to your wounds, but you must. Even if you think your wound is no big deal or just a "small cut" (hurt feelings), it's still important that you address it and monitor it closely. Just because it started off minor doesn't mean it won't escalate to something major.

Let me give you a couple of examples to help you understand what I mean. Let's say you asked to be on the praise team at church. If you weren't chosen to sing, your feelings may be hurt initially (minor cut) but as time goes on, you begin to develop feelings of resentment because you did not address the hurt (pray). Now, you have become bitter toward everyone who sings. You may even visit another church and hear someone singing, but find that you can't receive this person's vocal ministry because you have not gotten over feeling rejected (deep wound). If you had taken the matter to God, He would have revealed all your impure motives. I say "impure" because people generally get upset about things like this when their hearts are not in the right place, i.e., when they can't carry out their own agendas in ministry. (Ministry should never be used to bring attention to yourself.)

Another example of an untreated mental/emotional wound: Let's say someone you knew hosted an event, and you were not invited. You feel left out (minor cut). You never took that hurt to God, so, when the person hosts another event and invites you this time, you refuse to go because you haven't forgiven them for not inviting you to the last event. Not only are you against attending this new event, you have resolved not to attend *any* of this person's future events. You convince yourself that no one wants you around, so you become isolated. Whenever someone talks about going to an event or outing, your response is, "I don't know if I'm invited." You have developed a negative attitude and are easily offended.

Do you see how something minor can quickly turn into something major? Even the smallest wound requires attention. People walk around every day bleeding internally. This hemorrhaging becomes obvious when they blow up or suffer a nervous breakdown. The wound (violation) has eaten them up from the inside out.

A bleeding wound only gets worse as it continues to bleed. It contaminates your character, making you agitated and mean. Whereas you may have once been loving and sweet, you end up hateful and bitter. The unhealthy emotions I have mentioned throughout this book will become spirits that will follow you around like a shadow. The spirit of resentment, the spirit of unforgiveness, the spirit of anger, the spirit of frustration, the spirit of bitterness, and the spirit of depression will go wherever you go. You might change friends, jobs, churches or even spouses. But if your wound is still bleeding and you have not cast down these spirits, I assure you that every affiliation you have will be sabotaged and you will be hindered from knowing God (2 Cor. 10:5, NLT).

Some of us have become so immune to the pain from our old wound, we don't consider it to be a problem. We've simply grown accustomed to living with it. Know that even if the pain of your wound is no longer obvious, it still needs attention.

I remember being at the dentist's office once and being told I needed to have an infected tooth pulled. I told the dentist that I would wait a while, since the tooth wasn't hurting. She told me, "Just because it's not causing problems now doesn't mean it won't cause problems for you later." I needed to get the infected tooth out of my body, she said, because it could spread to other areas. I learned that what could be a simple dental procedure if done in time could easily turn into a hospital stay … or much worse … if ignored.

Never procrastinate on addressing your emotional wound. Do not make excuses for failing to do so. Humble yourself and take the issue to God in prayer. Confess your sins and repent. Renounce pride, rebellion and stubbornness. Cry out to God, letting Him know that you want the bleeding to stop. Forgive and pray for everyone who has hurt you; they probably have no idea what they did to you. Hand over to God all pain, guilt, shame, rejection, betrayal, trauma, and abuse. Let go of hatred, resentment and thoughts of revenge. I know it's difficult, because we tend to use what hurts us as a crutch to justify our negative actions. But forgiving those who hurt you is so much better than a crutch – it's healing!

As you forgive those who hurt you, ask God to forgive you. Some of us are willing participants in our own destruction. Not all our wounds are caused by others; some are caused by us. These wounds may not be deadly, but they're still self-inflicted. For instance, you suffer from an illness because you refuse to change your diet. You're worried and depressed because you can't manage and maintain the lifestyle you have created. You're unhappy in a relationship because you ignored all the red flags raised by the other person's actions. These are things for which you *must* take responsibility without falling into self-pity (another self-destructive behavior).

Now each of us will experience adversity. Bad things *will* happen, and they don't just happen to bad people. We are not exempt from tragedy. It's O.K. to be upset, and even cry. You have to cry in order to feel a little bit lighter. Dr. William H. Frey III, Ph.D., a neuroscientist, says that "not only is crying a human response to sorrow and frustration, it's a healthy one. Crying is a natural way to reduce emotional stress that causes cardiovascular disease and other stress-related disorders." I've heard older people all my life say, "You better cry before you make yourself sick." On the other hand, they'll say, "You better *stop* all that crying before you make yourself sick." What I've gathered from this is, it's just as necessary to *stop* crying as it is to *start*. So, go ahead and cry if you need to. However, at some point, you must pull yourself together and move past the crying so that you won't become consumed by the pain. Never let your emotions get out of control. (Remember my friend's crying, paranoid friend in the "Swim Away" chapter?)

Even tears of joy can come from a place of sorrow and grief. Let me explain. When my son Sirrod graduated from high school, I was beyond excited; I was extremely proud. At the same time, I felt bad for him because of an ordeal he had gone through with another person shortly before his graduation. As he walked across the stage, my tears began to fall. I was trying to keep my emotions *and* satan in check. The enemy will use any opportunity possible to rob you of your joy. He wants to turn your happy tears into tears of sadness. His goal is to kill, steal, and destroy. As you go through the adversities of life, never forget satan's intent.

Evil Soul Ties

Some wounds, as well as demonic spirits, come from evil soul ties. These are idols in our lives that take our focus off God. These soul ties are formed out of past or present relationships and affiliations. The effects of being intertwined with the wrong people and things can be as lethal as a venomous snake. These ties poison your spirit and cause you to disconnect from God – *"for 'bad company corrupts good character'"* (1 Cor. 15:33b. NLT). Just know that whatever and whoever comes between you and God is a problem. Those ties need to be cut.

If you are depressed and harboring thoughts of suicide, check your soul ties. Those feelings can be a direct result of who, or what, you're connected to. Can you think of a person who brings out the worst in you? The *closer* you are to this person, the *further* you feel from God. Atrocious demonic spirits use ungodly soul ties to get to you and keep you from loving God wholeheartedly. You must come to terms with the fact that some people and things are not good for you.

If you are struggling emotionally and don't understand why, start looking for answers. **I believe the first place you should look is within yourself, but don't ever forget to look at the people and things you're connected to. It could be an evil soul tie that's causing your dysfunction.** It might be someone who calls you often. You care about them, but you know they are bitter and showing signs of an evil spirit. Don't view this person's call as a simple phone call. It's much more serious than that. Think of the conversation as the vehicle used by an evil spirit to get to you. Spirits are relentless. They do not go away easy. You must be just as determined for the spirit to *leave* you as it is determined to *stay*. Have you ever noticed that the most evil person in churches never leaves? The reason is because the spirit controlling that person doesn't want him or her to go. It has manipulated that person, and now wants to control everyone else in the church. This person might come week after week and sit with a countenance that says, "I dare you to confront me." The spirit is trying to intimidate you so that you won't address it. You cannot be afraid when dealing with evil spirits. If you don't call them out, they will *never* leave you alone.

Spirits are real, and you should be aware of this every day of your life. Even when a foul spirit has entered your home, drive it right back out with the authority that God has given you. Declare that you will have peace in your home. When a spirit attacks your emotions, don't try to be nice – command that depression, that bitterness, that guilt, that shame to **LEAVE!** Once the spirit is gone, replace it with good habits and Christlike behaviors*: "You were taught, with regard to your former way of life, to put off your old self, which is being corrupted by its deceitful desires; to be made new in the attitude of your minds"* (Ephesians 4:22-23, NIV).

When I moved to Atlanta, I noticed that several homes had yard signs that read "private residence." That means you are not allowed on this property if you were not invited. You need to have the same mentality of a homeowner displaying such a sign! Let evil spirits know they are not welcome.

If you have accepted Jesus as Lord of your life, you can be sure of victory over these demons. There is no need to fear evil spirits when you have been filled with the Holy Spirit! With God, you can live free from emotional bondage and spiritual distress. Seek to dwell in God's presence. Ungodly spirits cannot abide there. In His presence is where wounds you thought would never stop bleeding will begin to heal.

PRAYER

"When the Wounds Won't Heal"

Dear Lord,

I come under Your authority and Your claim on my life. Thank You for being a healer of all wounds. I can't fix my wounds, but I know You can. I give myself to You – mind, body and spirit. Recover the pieces of my broken heart, and make me whole again. Remove sadness and grief, and replace it with peace and joy. Help me to forgive every offense caused by others as well as myself. Forgive me for the way I mishandled my brokenness. I renounce sin and ungodly connections. Lord, I welcome Your healing. Renew my spirit and restore my soul. Amen

– 11 –
In Ruins

My suffering was good for me, for it taught me to pay attention to your decrees. Your instructions are more valuable to me than millions in gold and silver.

(Psalm 119:71-72, NLT)

In 1993, as a fifteen-year-old who had just completed middle school, I visited twenty-one countries in Europe. I was one of a group of about eight students and two chaperones. We were all excited about our international trip. Our first stop was London, then to Paris to see the Eiffel Tower. We also toured Italy, visiting the Leaning Tower of Pisa, the Vatican and the Roman ruins.

Of all our travel destinations, one place sticks out in my mind: the Colosseum in Rome, also known as the Flavian Amphitheater. The largest amphitheater ever built, it was almost destroyed by earthquakes and stone robbers. Although it is in ruins, it's still one of Rome's most popular tourist attractions. The people of the city never reconstructed the Colosseum, nor did they tear it down. They just preserved what was left. This monument consists of millions of broken stones and concrete, but it is still an amazing site. People from all over the world travel to Rome to see a structure that is partially collapsed!

I believe there is a message in all things, including the Colosseum. I couldn't see that as a teenager. But now that I have been shaken by my own personal earthquakes, I understand the message: All of us have had times when our lives were in a total mess. Everything was out of place, and it seemed that God was O.K. with it being that way.

Just like the monument in Rome, you were in ruins. **God won't always put people and things back together again; He'll sometimes allow everything to fall apart ... and let it remain that way.** Sometimes, God can use you better in pieces. When He needs you to be His advertisement, He might not want every part of you to be well put together. He needs the world to see that He can use flawed people to carry out His plan. Oftentimes, we're worried about what we look like, and what people will think of our mess. But God can make our ruins attractive to people. Remember Paul's "thorn in the flesh" (2 Corinthians 12:7-10)?

Sometimes, God can use you better in pieces.

When we visited Pisa, Italy, we were amazed at the Leaning Tower. Hundreds of people were standing around, staring at it. The tilt was caused by a faulty foundation during the tower's construction. The ground was too soft on one side, and could not support the structure's weight. It appeared as though the tower was going to fall. Just like some of us. We're leaning, but we're still standing.

Rome's Flavian Amphitheater is completely exposed on one side. It was broken in pieces, but the remaining part still stands strong. It has drawn more people since the earthquake than it did before.

Exposure

You may have experienced your own personal disaster. The enemy meant it for evil, but God will always work it out for your good and His glory.

Exposure for a Christian never feels good. I've had my experience with it, and it's the worst I've ever felt. In fact, it seemed worse than death at the time because it was a deliberate and elaborate attempt to destroy my reputation. My personal business was put on the street, embellished with lies. People believed the lies and persecuted me because of them. For the believer, there is hope even in death, but I felt hopeless. Like the Roman ruins, I was in shambles. The worst part was the betrayal by people I trusted. It's much easier to get over the remarks and actions of someone you don't know. The damage caused by those you thought were loyal to you is devastating. Those are the wounds that don't heal easily.

Another reason exposure can hurt so bad is because a lot of what's being said is not a lie. Some of it is the truth, but **no one wants their truth (business) told without their permission.** The truth hurts, but lies do too. The lies added to the truth are what keeps you angry. Can you see how your emotions are all over the place? You're brokenhearted, embarrassed, hurt, sad, angry, and frustrated. You want to lash out, but you're trying to salvage what's left of your character. So, you remain silent. It's a painful position to be in. Your life looks like the Amphitheater. One side is exposed, and the other side is intact.

As I pointed out earlier, the earthquake was not the only thing that damaged the Amphitheater; stone robbers made off with pieces of the structure. Those missing pieces contributed to the disaster as well. (You must be on guard for the "stone robbers" in your life – the people who will take pieces of you and leave you to fall apart.)

With exposure, people typically only see one side. To this day, most of the people who visit the Colosseum, or look at pictures of it, still don't know what really happened. The incredible thing is that the ruined part of the structure is the part everyone wants to see. It's what makes it world renowned.

When I look back over my life and think about all the damage and pain caused by others as well as myself, I understand God's purpose for it all. It took many years for me to get it, but I finally do: **When God draws us unto Him, we don't get to decide how He does it. He might use our ruins to carry out His plan.** So, don't despise your past. The effects of the earthquake almost demolished the Colosseum, but the damage is what makes it relevant today.

There was another dreadful event that took place long ago. It was the most memorable event in the history of Christianity. It was when Jesus suffered and died on the cross for our sins, then rose from the grave three days later. Because of His sacrifice, each of us is justified, relevant, and useful.

And as people who are reconciled to God through His Son, we can be assured that there is always a connection between our *pain* and our *purpose*. Because I have dealt with the heartache of my life being exposed, I can help someone going through a similar situation. It's my belief that you cannot effectively minister to people who are broken if you have never been broken yourself. There are certain people only *you* can reach. Your story, suffering and tears included, is a part of God's plan. You know more about Him after your disaster than you did before. Now, you can tell someone else that you know God to be a healer, keeper, burden bearer, deliverer, and so much more … He will reveal things to you in your broken state that you couldn't see when you were complete. Some lessons are only learned through pain.

If your life ends up in ruins, look for God in the rubble. Never forget who you are and *whose* you are. Remember that your problem did not come to defeat you, it came to develop you. Just as hail forms only in thunderstorms, some things develop within us only during the storms of life.

Be confident in knowing that however God decides to fix your situation, it's for sure the best way it could have been done. Be confident, as the three young Hebrew men were confident in the face of what seemed to be certain death after refusing to worship the golden image set up by the Babylonian King Nebuchadnezzar:

> **If it be so, our God whom we serve is able to deliver us from the burning fiery furnace, and he will deliver us out of thine hand, O king. But if not, let it be known unto thee, O king, that we will not serve thy gods, nor worship the golden image which thou hast set up. (Daniel 3:17-18, KJV)**

PRAYER
"In Ruins"

Dear Lord,

Thank You for every trial that made me stronger. Keep my mind when everything around me is falling apart. Help me to depend on You to fix it *Your* way. When I feel stripped of everything, cover me with Your grace and Your mercy. Protect me from the hand of the enemy. Thank You for all the pieces You did *not* put back together. I trust Your plan and purpose for my life. Use my ruins to bring Your name glory. Thank You for showing Yourself strong and mighty in my weakness. I'm forever grateful for Your love, kindness and faithfulness. Amen

– 12 –

THE SIGNIFICANCE OF THE CROSS

For God so loved the world, that He gave His only begotten Son, that whosoever believeth in him should not perish, but have everlasting life.

(John 3:16, KJV)

The cross signifies pain, torture and torment. There is a line in the hymn "The Old Rugged Cross" that defines it as "an emblem of suffering and shame." When you think of the cross as it relates to Calvary, you know that this was certainly no symbol of comfort, pleasure or merriment.

In ancient times, actual crosses were used for executions, so you should never take your figurative cross lightly. When Jesus told His disciples to "take up your cross, and follow me," He meant that the disciples had to be willing to die to themselves in order to follow Him (Luke 9:23-25). When Jesus was on His way to be crucified, He had to carry His own execution device (cross) to Golgotha. Many theologians argue that the cross represents a weight, a burden to carry. But it can't be argued that the cross is a symbol of death: For the disciples, the cross meant "to die for Christ." For Christ, the cross meant "to die for us all." That Jesus died so that we might live is not up for debate. (At least not with me it isn't!)

For the disciples, the cross meant "to die for Christ." For Christ, the cross meant "to die for us all."

Following Jesus requires complete sacrifice. In John 16:33, Jesus assured us that trials will come to those who commit themselves to the will of God. Discipleship is not a walk in the park. A life without pain and suffering was never promised. Each of us has a cross to bear. It may be the cross of sickness/disease, the cross of divorce, the cross of financial hardship, or the cross of sorrow/grief. According to *McGraw-Hill Dictionary of American Idioms and Phrasal Verbs*, to bear a cross is to accept an unpleasant situation or responsibility because you can't change it. But all is not lost; Jesus says in the last part of Verse 33 to "be of good cheer; I have overcome the world." Just because you can't change your situation doesn't mean God can't!

> *Just because you can't change your situation doesn't mean God can't!*

Now there will be times when God will allow you to carry your cross because there's a lesson in your distress. The heaviness of the cross can become overwhelming; some of the problems you encounter will seem so unnecessary. In those times, ask God for more grace to carry your cross. I know you want your suffering to end, but there is a divine purpose for your pain.

Remember the 2004 movie *The Passion of The Christ*, which included very graphic scenes of the last 12 hours of Jesus' life? If you saw it, chances are you desperately wanted to get to the resurrection scene. But the resurrection could not happen without the crucifixion. It was gruesome, but it was necessary. Fast-forward to your cross-bearing process, during which you might stumble and fall. Although it's torturous and seems pointless, there's a reason for it all. According to doctrinal belief, Jesus fell three times while carrying the cross down the painful path of the Via Dolorosa. These places were called the "stations of the cross." The point that I'm trying to convey is, even the places where Jesus fell were significant.

> *Even the places where Jesus fell were significant.*

For you, it may have gone beyond *carrying* the cross – you may now feel as though you're *nailed* to the cross. It can be a humiliating place. People will taunt you. Friends will become few; they may flee or watch from a distance like they did the day Jesus was crucified. You may even be alienated from family members. Some will question God's love for you. But you must develop and maintain a **stay-on-the-cross mentality.** You must endure the brutal taunts of the enemy. Drawing on God's Spirit, rather than your might or power (Zechariah 4:6), you can!

As Jesus suffered on the cross, the mockers told Him to come down and prove his identity: *"Well then, save yourself, and come down from the cross"* (Mark 15:30, NLT). But He did not come down. He sacrificed His life for us. Here's how you apply this concept to your everyday life. You don't have to combat every negative remark made to or about you. Remain silent and let your *life* speak for you. Jesus was the perfect example of loving tolerance. He took the pain, endured the suffering, accepted the agony and died … then, He rose. Even if He had never declared that all power was in His hands (Matthew 28:18), the fact that He got up said it all! His life spoke for Him.

So, don't become distracted by people. You must be confident in knowing that the God in you is much bigger than what people say or do. The effectiveness of Jesus' blood has not changed. It was powerful then, and it's just as powerful today. His blood has the power to heal you, deliver you from all hurt and harm, and set you free. There will be people you'll encounter who will make every attempt to draw you away from God, but you must stay focused on the things of God. You have a calling on your life and a specific assignment to complete.

As dreadful as it may be, it's important that you stay on the cross you've borne. The cross seemed final for Jesus, but it wasn't the end for Him; just as the cross wasn't the end for Jesus, it's not the end for you. There is nothing you have done that Jesus did not consider when He hung on His cross. He took into consideration your family, your flaws, and whatever issue you are struggling with. He thought of it all. He was innocent, but He chose to suffer and die so that you could live. He went through all this because He loves you so much. There is no one who loves you like Jesus does! No one else is so gracious and forgiving.

> *There is nothing you have done that Jesus did not consider when He hung on His cross.*

If you are at a place in your life where you're questioning God's love for you, the answer is at the cross. Take a moment and imagine Jesus hanging there, His back ripped open like a plowed field against an old rugged cross to which His hands and feet had been nailed. The weight of His body was so heavy that He had to struggle for every breath, pushing up against the cross with His open flesh. He was beaten so badly that His body was covered in blood. The Roman soldiers mocked Jesus and tortured Him further by making a crown out of sharp branches that we call thorns, and pressing it upon His head.

> *If you are at a place in your life where you're questioning God's love for you, the answer is at the cross.*

Many artists have painted pictures of Jesus on the cross, but none of them can show what Jesus really looked like at that time. According to Isaiah 52:14, *"many were amazed when they saw him. His face was so disfigured he seemed hardly human, and from his appearance, one would scarcely know he was a man"* (NLT). They even pierced Him in the side with a spear, as a hunter would pierce a wild animal, and blood and water came gushing out. (The water is said to have been built-up fluid in his lungs and chest due to shock and massive blood loss.)

There was nothing pleasant about the cross. It was disturbing and brutal. Yet, Jesus prayed, asking God to forgive His tormentors.

Your mind and spirit might be under attack right now. If so, I plead with you to reflect on the cross. Pondering the magnitude of what took place on Calvary gives you a better understanding of Jesus' love for you. Many of us have a tough time letting go of even a small piece of what we love for the sake of someone else, but God gave His only Son so that we could have eternal life.

The enemy wants you to believe you are worthless, that your life has no meaning. There will be days when you wake up and wonder "Why am I still here?" You may feel completely insignificant. When these thoughts raid your mind, and satan tries to convince you that you don't belong here, put your mind right back on Calvary. Picture Jesus hanging on the cross in agony, drenched in blood, struggling to breathe. Remember that He adores you. With every whip, nail, thorn and drop of blood that was shed, He had you on His mind. Others may have started off loving you, only for their love to fade away. Jesus' love does not diminish. He loves you just as much today as He did the day He died on the cross.

PRAYER

"The Significance of the Cross"

Dear Lord,

Thank You for dying in my place. All the torture You endured was meant for me. My heart is grateful for the love that was shown at Calvary. Nothing and no one can compare to You. You are my greatest example of tolerance. The afflictions of this world cannot equate to the agony You suffered.

Thank You for giving me the strength to bear my cross. Help me to cast down thoughts of worthlessness and be confident in knowing that You considered me worth saving. My desire is to live a life that brings You glory. Teach me how to always speak to the dead things in my life, and faithfully wait on their resurrection. Amen

- 13 -
THE EMPTY GRAVE

They found the stone rolled away from the tomb, but when they entered, they did not find the body of the Lord Jesus.

(Luke 24:2-3, NIV)

In the time that it has taken you to read this book, satan has talked someone into taking their life. You are still here, and still reading, so that gives me a little more time to convince you to live. You might be thinking that you'd never get low enough to shoot yourself or jump from a bridge. The fact of the matter is, if you are full of hate, rage, bitterness, unforgiveness or any other unhealthy emotion, you *are* killing yourself … you just chose a different way to do it. Your way might not be as violent, but it's just as tragic.

You may be feeling weak because life has taken its toll on you, but you are stronger than you think. It takes strength to deal with the kind of pain and torment you have suffered through. Just the fact that you decided to read a book about preventing self-destruction means you want to live! God has so much more for you to do. Don't believe satan when he tries to tell you that you are worthless and have no purpose here. Your life has meaning. Jesus showed you how much on Calvary.

William J. Gaither wrote a song that tells of Jesus' love for you. You may have heard it sung since your childhood days in church. But you may have not paid real attention to the words, or considered how they relate to your current situation. As you read, let the lyrics minister to you.

Because He Lives

God sent His Son, they called Him Jesus;
He came to love, heal, and forgive;
He lived and died to buy my pardon,
An empty grave is there to prove my Savior lives!

**Because He lives, I can face tomorrow,
Because He lives, all fear is gone,
Because I know He holds the future,
And life is worth the living,
Just because He lives!**

The empty grave, too powerful to deny, confirms that Jesus is ALIVE!

Whatever you are faced with in life, always remember how far Jesus went to prove His love for you. At the same time, never lose sight of satan's deep commitment to keeping you from living a fulfilled life. None of his attacks will come by surprise when you are fully aware of his objective. He wants to go beyond hurting you; he wants to kill you.

The enemy began plotting against me at an early age. Since the first time Madear (my grandmother) told me this story, I have asked her many times to share it again.

One evening, when I was four or five months old, my grandmother babysat me. After returning to pick me up, my parents had fallen asleep in the living room. Madear was in one of the bedrooms at the back of the house, enjoying her time with me. She had been talking, singing, and playing with me for hours. She said I was jolly as ever, giggling and kicking like babies do. Suddenly, my head tilted back and my body went limp. My eyes were slightly open, but I wasn't blinking. I didn't make a sound. She lifted my head and realized that I had stopped breathing completely.

Madear immediately began to pray. While pleading with God, she tried everything she could to get me to show some sign of life. Nothing she tried was working. Several minutes went by; I still was not breathing. She told me how it seemed like forever that she worked with me, trying to get a response. Realizing there was nothing else she could do to bring me back, she asked God, "How am I going to tell Dorris and Edward that their baby is gone?" She was so weak she could hardly walk, but she knew she had to let them know. So, she started heading toward the hallway with my lifeless body in her arms.

When Madear made it to the next bedroom door, she said, "Come on, Lisha, breathe." Nothing happened. By the time she'd almost reached the living room, I still wasn't breathing. She stopped one last time and said, "God, please bring her back. I don't want to tell them that their baby is dead." Still no response from me. With tears in her eyes, she kept walking. Just as she was about to show my parents my body, I let out a long sigh – "Aaaaaaahhhhhh" – and I began to breathe.

She thought it was over, Madear told me, but God cancelled the devil's plans! It wasn't time for me to die. I had a purpose to fulfill, children to raise, books to write, gifts to use and ministry to carry out … and satan has been out to get me ever since that day at Madear's house. He's enraged that God let me live. He thought he had won. He has tried time and time again to redeem himself for such a major loss, but he can't have me. I'm in the safety of the Lord: *"He that dwelleth in the secret place of the most high shall abide under the shadow of the Almighty. I will say of the LORD, He is my refuge and my fortress; my God; in him will I trust"* (Psalm 91:1-2, KJV).

Think of a time when satan tried to take you out, but God stepped in just in time. The enemy may have changed his tactics. He may be attacking your mind right now with thoughts of suicide and feelings of hopelessness and grief. Remember that God has given you the power and authority to rebuke the devil in Jesus' name and cast down those imaginations (2 Cor. 10:5)!

I know it seems final, but it's not over until God says it's over. Keep moving, even when it seems easier to just stop. No matter how long you've been in a low place, just know that God can turn your situation around in an instant. If you are debating whether you should live or die, I plead with you to **choose life!** Let God finish what He started in you: *"And I am certain that God, who began the good work within you, will continue his work until it is finally finished on the day when Jesus Christ returns"* (Philippians 1:6, NLT).

> *Keep moving, even when it seems easier to just stop.*

Live Well

Death has been cancelled! The hit has been called off! Now, it's time to live the life that God intended. I've listed six strategies to promote a lifetime of productivity.

- **First, develop a will to live.** Without it, you'll reject everything that life has to offer. You have to *want* to be here, and be willing to endure every situation you encounter. For example: You might have a good spouse who is kind, attentive, and caters to your every need. But if you don't want that spouse, nothing he or she does or provides will ever mean anything to you. Just like the person in an unwanted marriage, you will be miserable living an unwanted life.

- **Prioritize your life.** Put everyone and everything in its proper place. Use your time and energy wisely. Don't waste precious time on things that bring no value to your life and to the kingdom of God.
- **Pursue God's purpose for your life.** God had a plan for you even before you were born. It's important to Him that you fulfill your God-given purpose before you leave this earth.
- **Become motivated by your possibilities.** Give yourself permission to be excited about what *could* be. Your possibilities are what drive you. Don't let fear hinder you from living a fulfilled life.
- **Surround yourself with positive, forward-thinking people.** Positive people not only want the best for themselves, they want the best for you as well. Their positive energy will transfer to you.
- **Live life without limits!** Imagine your feet being cemented to the ground. It would be impossible for you to take steps. You would be able to lean and reach, but only while standing in the same spot.

That's what living a life with limits is like. Many of the limits on your life are limits *you* placed there. You can't control what others do, but you have complete control of what you do to yourself. Sometimes, it's not what you do at all, it's what you *think*. You must free yourself from the bondage of your own mind. You must be uncompromisingly determined to knock down every wall and break through every barrier (strongholds, generational curses, fear, etc.).

It's your choice. You make the call. You can either live your life bound up, or live it set free!

Prayer

"The Empty Grave"

Dear Lord,

Thank You for the gift of life. Help me to activate my faith and live out my purpose. Thank You for deciding to die, and rising three days later. The empty grave proves Your love for me. When I'm overwhelmed, saturate me with Your peace and love. Surround me with genuine people who care about my well-being. Teach me how to be productive and manage my time properly. Thank You for cancelling the enemy's plan. Lord, keep and cover me daily. Give me a fresh start and the courage to live my life without limits. Amen

BIBLIOGRAPHY

The Holy Bible. New Living Translation, 1996, New International Version, 1978, International Standard Version, 1998, King James Version 1611

Clark, Heather. "Georgia Pastor Commits Suicide Just Months After Stopping Man From Killing Himself." Christian News Network. N.p., 21 Nov. 2013. Web. 24 May 2017. <http://christiannews.net/2013/11/19/georgia-pastor-commits-suicide-just-months-after-stopping-man-from-killing-himself/>.

"Psychology Today: Solitude vs Loneliness." Psychology Today: Solitude vs Loneliness ~. N.p., n.d. Web. 24 May 2017. <http://wemustnotthinktoomuch.blogspot.com/2008/05/psychology-today-solitude-vs-loneliness.html>.

"Dictionary.com." Dictionary.com. Dictionary.com, n.d. Web. 24 May 2017. <http://www.dictionary.com/>.

Grewal, Daisy. "How Wealth Reduces Compassion." Scientific American. N.p., 09 Apr. 2012. Web. 24 May 2017. <https://www.scientificamerican.com/article/how-wealth-reduces-compassion/>.

"Schaeffer Institute." Into Thy Word Ministries. N.p., n.d. Web. 24 May 2017. <http://www.intothyword.org/pages.asp?pageid=53513>.

"Www.Followyourdreamfarm.net." Www. Followyourdreamfarm.net - Follow your dream farm. N.p., n.d. Web. 24 May 2017. <http://urlm.co/www.followyourdreamfarm.net>.

"McGraw-Hill's dictionary of American idioms and phrasal verbs." Find in a library with WorldCat. N.p., 01 Apr. 2017. Web. 24 May 2017. <http://www.worldcat.org/title/mcgraw-hills-dictionary-of-american-idioms-and-phrasal-verbs/oclc/56982023>.

"Bible Commentary - Matthew Henry Concise." Bible Study Tools. N.p., n.d. Web. 25 May 2017. <http://www.biblestudytools.com/commentaries/matthew-henry-concise/>.

www.ingramcontent.com/pod-product-compliance
Lightning Source LLC
LaVergne TN
LVHW051605070426
835507LV00021B/2774